IMAGES
of America

LA GRANGE

Located in central Texas along the Colorado River, La Grange is a mere 80 miles from the Gulf of Mexico. Its moderate climate and ample rainfall support rolling prairies and forested areas that are ideal for farming. A towering bluff along the Colorado River overlooks the town, as shown in this 1890s photograph. (Courtesy FPLMA.)

ON THE COVER: For more than 175 years, the Muster Oak has been a rallying point for La Grange citizens eager to fight for their beliefs. Military recruits from six conflicts gathered under its branches before going off to war. Located in the northeast corner of the town square, the tree, pictured in 1910, is recognized in *Famous Trees of Texas*. (Courtesy FPLMA.)

IMAGES
of America

LA GRANGE

Marie W. Watts

ARCADIA
PUBLISHING

Published by Arcadia Publishing
Charleston SC, Chicago IL, Portsmouth NH, San Francisco CA

Library of Congress Catalog Card Number: 2007943603

For all general information contact Arcadia Publishing at:
Telephone 843-853-2070
Fax 843-853-0044
E-mail sales@arcadiapublishing.com
For customer service and orders:
Toll-Free 1-888-313-2665

Visit us on the Internet at www.arcadiapublishing.com

*To my daughters, Kristin Higueros and Karen Lively, and to my
husband, Tim Nelsen. Without your love and support,
I could not have attempted this project.*

CONTENTS

ACKNOWLEDGMENTS

This book would not have been possible without the assistance of the Fayette Public Library, Museum, and Archives (FPLMA). Run by the City of La Grange, the organization is the guardian of thousands of historical images and documents, which were willingly shared with me. Archivists Donna Green and Sherie Knape patiently located photographs, answered questions, and shared stories, helping fill this work with interesting and poignant tales of the past. Library manager and historian Kathy Carter read the manuscript to ensure its accuracy. For this support, I am eternally grateful.

Other area museums were also a great help. Special thanks go to Dennis Ed Smith of the Monument Hill and Kreische Brewery State Historic Site and to Aina Dodge of the Texas Parks and Wildlife Department for assistance in locating photographs of the Kreische Brewery and the Scheutzenverein. Thanks also go to the following organizations: the La Grange Garden Club, which runs the Faison House Museum; the Railroad Museum; the Old Jail Museum, and the Czech Heritage and Cultural Center.

And last but not least, thanks to acquisitions editor Kristie Kelly of Arcadia Publishing, who acted as cheerleader and editor, and to my daughter Karen Lively, who worked on the images and helped in the text assembly.

INTRODUCTION

La Grange is as bold as the state itself. Before the town was founded, Native Americans lived and traded in the area, as La Grange is located near one of the few low-water crossings on the Colorado River. Spanish and French explorers later traversed the vicinity on La Bahía Road, which also crossed the Colorado at the ford.

By the early 1820s, a few hardy Anglo settlers were making their way to the area. Encouraged by land grants issued by Stephen F. Austin, 22 colonists settled in and near La Grange, the westernmost outpost of Austin's colony. By the early 1830s, most of the Tonkawa, Lipan, and Comanche Indians had been forced out of the area, and citizens turned to another war: the War for Texas Independence. La Grange residents figured prominently in the struggle against the Mexicans, and many ran for their lives ahead of Santa Anna's army in what is now called the Runaway Scrape.

After independence, citizens continued to do their share to keep the republic free. Meeting under the Muster Oak, they rode off to fight against two of the Mexican incursions of 1842—though with disastrous consequences. Heroes of the conflicts the Dawson Massacre and the Mier Expedition are buried at the Monument Hill and Kreische State Historical Site, just outside of La Grange.

When Texas president Sam Houston vetoed the bill making La Grange the capital of the Republic of Texas, livid citizens issued a bill of indictment against the government. Soon, however, they settled down to making money. La Grange served as the seat for Fayette County and as a center of commerce for the area's population. Land was cheap and plentiful, and before long, cotton became king. Slaves, who were needed to tend the cash crop, quickly made up 33 percent of the county's population.

During this time, German and Czech immigrants tired of famines, conscriptions, expensive land, and constant European wars also flooded the area. Because of their influence, Fayette County was one of the few in Texas to vote against secession. Despite the no confidence vote, many area citizens took up the Confederate cause. The war, however, devastated the economy, and the Reconstruction years took a terrible toll on La Grange citizens. Cotton and corn continued to be cash crops but were raised on small farms rather than plantations.

By the end of the 19th century, 25 percent of the county's population was foreign born and Fayette County boasted newspapers in both Czech and German. The hardworking, beer-loving immigrants organized social clubs and attended dances as a break from their hardscrabble life. During the 20th century, oil, cattle, and other natural resources gradually became mainstays of the La Grange economy. From the 1940s through the 1970s, the population of the county dropped precipitously, as residents who could no longer earn a living on the farm moved to the big city.

A brothel on the outskirts of town quietly contributed to the area's economy until 1973, when it was closed down by Houston television reporter Marvin Zindler. The Chicken Ranch, to the horror of the citizens of La Grange, became known around the world, thanks to the play and movie *The Best Little Whorehouse in Texas*.

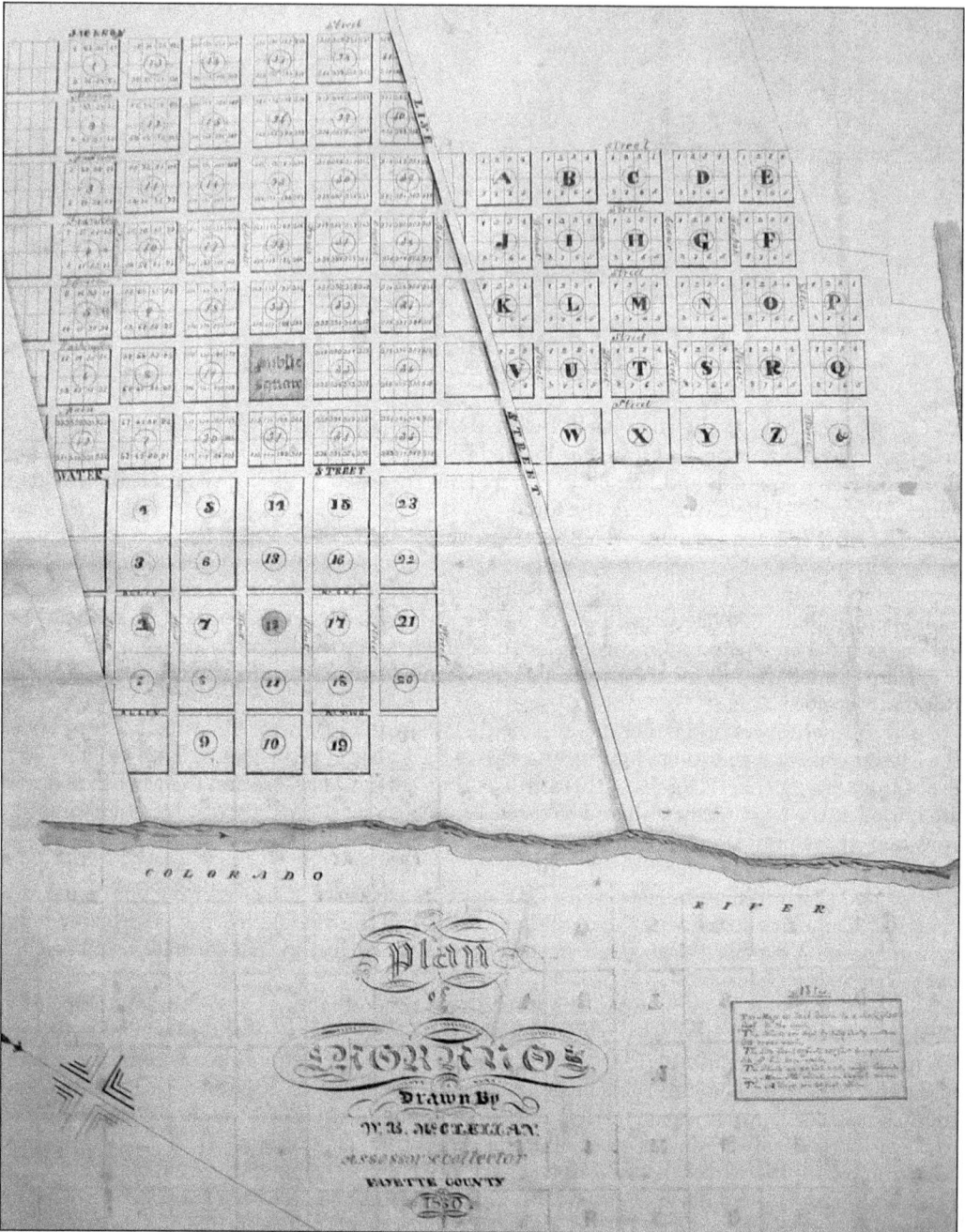

Land in 19th-century Texas was plentiful and inexpensive. The founders of La Grange, expecting many newcomers who coveted land, laid out a Texas-sized town. Shown here is the 1850 plat of the town along the banks of the Colorado River in Fayette County. (Courtesy Texas State Library and Archives Commission.)

One

NATIVE AMERICANS AND THE SEVEN FLAGS OVER LA GRANGE

Native Americans populated the La Grange area 8,000 to 12,000 years ago because it afforded these hunter-gatherers plentiful game and water. They used the area as a neutral place for living and trading. By the 1800s, the main tribes in the La Grange area were the Tonkawas, the Comanches, and the Lipan Apaches.

The Spanish (1519–1685; 1690–1821) were the first to invade what is now Texas and claim the La Grange area for themselves. Along with the immigrants who followed, they brought disease, epidemics, and other hardships to the Native Americans. From 1492 to 1900, it is estimated that the Native American population in Texas decreased by 90 percent. The French (1685–1690) also planted their flag in Texas—at Fort St. Louis, about 100 miles from La Grange. By 1690, the settlement was abandoned and the French attempt at colonization ended.

The next flag to grace the area was that of Mexico (1821–1836), whose citizens were described as *Tejano*, Spanish for Texian. During this period, Anglo settlers from the United States began to move into the area. These settlers, increasingly unhappy with Mexican control in part because they had to embrace the Catholic religion and were not permitted to own slaves, revolted and formed the Republic of Texas (1836–1845). Mexico, however, sought to fight the rebellious Texians (as the residents of Texas liked to call themselves) and began making incursions into the state in the 1840s. Texas sought protection by joining the Union and has remained part of the United States since 1845—that is, except for the period from 1861 to 1865 when it was a member of the Confederate States of America.

One additional flag has flown over La Grange. While not that of a sovereign nation, the *Frisch Auf!* flag plays an important role in the history of the area.

La Grange, the real capital of Texas, is located in Fayette County, in the central part of the state. In 1838, the Republic of Texas approved the formation of the county, which is named in honor of Frenchman Gilbert du Motier, the Marquis de Lafayette and a popular Revolutionary War hero. The town of La Grange was laid out in 1837 on half a league of land granted to John H. Moore and bears the name of Lafayette's country estate. La Grange is now a bustling town of more than 4,600 that also serves as the county seat. The Fayette Public Library, Museum, and Archives proudly displays the six national flags of Texas to remind residents of the cultural influences that have made La Grange what it is today. (Courtesy author.)

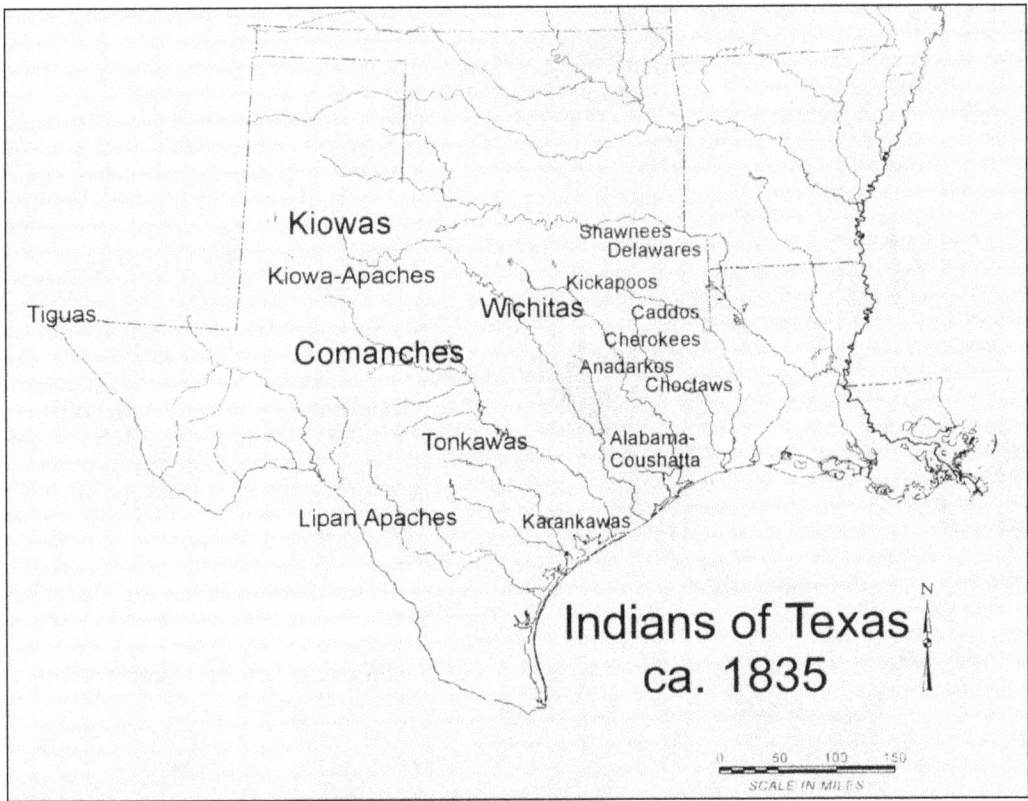

Indians of Texas ca. 1835

At first, the Tonkawas and Lipan Apaches welcomed the Anglos into central Texas, seeing them as a means to defeat their enemy to the north: the Comanches. They willingly served as army scouts and auxiliaries. Relationships with the Anglos deteriorated for the Tonkawas, however. By 1859, they had been moved into the Native American Territory, which is now Oklahoma. (Courtesy *The Texas Indians* by David La Vere, Texas A&M University Press, c. 2004.)

La Bahía Road was an east-west Native American trail that eventually ran from southeastern Texas, extending to Washington-on-the-Brazos and Goliad. It crossed the Colorado River near La Grange. The route was known as early as 1690, when it was traveled by Alonso De León. It later became a main artery to San Antonio and points beyond.

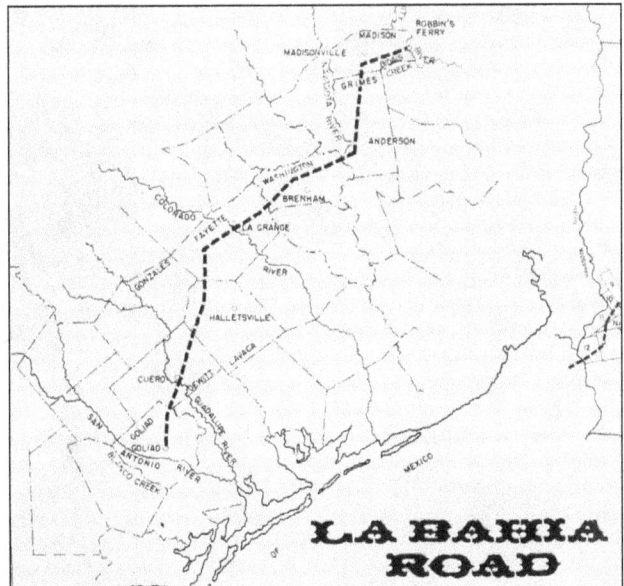

LA BAHIA ROAD

11

The Comanches, in particular, clashed with early settlers. Rachel Newman, the daughter of William Rabb, who brought his family to the area in 1823, reportedly had several skirmishes with them. Log cabin doors frequently did not touch the floor; when one Native American brave stuck his toes through the opening while trying to lift the door off its hinges, Rachel cut two of them off with an ax. Another time, she burned feather pillows in the fireplace to keep Comanche braves from coming down the chimney. The Comanche threat to La Grange ended in 1840 when Col. John H. Moore led an expedition against them at the Red Fork of the Colorado River, north of La Grange. During the Red Fork Massacre, Moore and his party of settlers killed 125 men, women, and children, took 34 captives, and, after burning the village, seized more than 500 horses. Shown here are George Catlin's sketches of Comanche chiefs, produced in 1835.

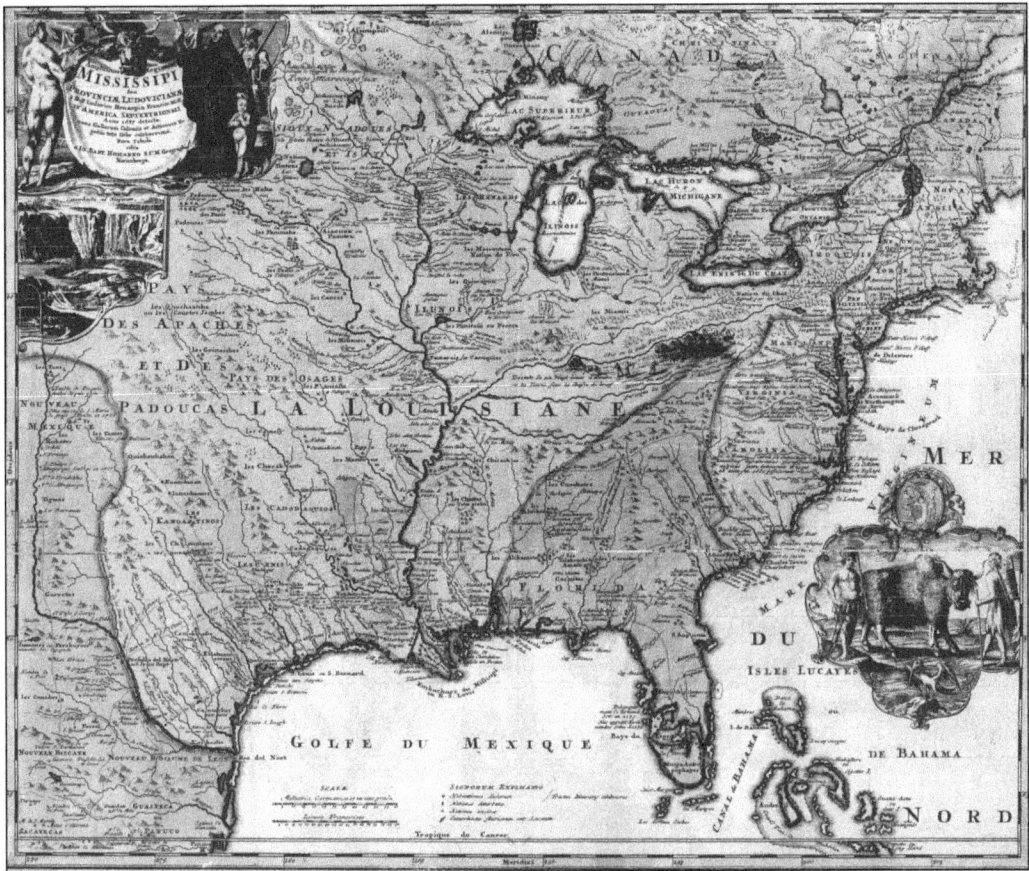

Seeking the Mississippi River, René-Robert Cavelier, the Sieur de La Salle, mistakenly landed on the Texas coastline at Matagorda Bay on February 20, 1685. His last passage at La Grange was made in February 1687. He stopped for several days in the area to visit with Native American tribes and to hunt. By March 19, La Salle was dead—a victim of assassination. His death and the massacre of the remaining French adults at Fort St. Louis ended French rule in Texas. At right, La Salle and his men unload ships in Texas. The map above is dated 1720 and entitled *Ampilssima Regionis Mississipi Seu Provinciae Ludoviciane* (Amplified Region of the Mississippi of the Province of Louisiana). (Above courtesy Texas State Library and Archives Commission; right courtesy Library of Congress.)

Alonso De León (below), the Spanish governor of Coahuila, led his fourth expedition into Texas in 1689, during which time he discovered the remains of La Salle's Fort St. Louis and passed through the La Grange area on La Bahía Road. The map at left, dated 1807, depicts the internal provinces of New Spain. (Left courtesy Texas State Library and Archives Commission; below courtesy Jack Edward Jackson estate.)

In 1821, Mexico won its independence from Spain, but the struggle left the country economically devastated. Desperate to protect itself from American expansion, the new Mexican government felt that the colonization of Texas would create a buffer zone. The Spanish government gave Moses Austin a contract to establish a colony of 300 Catholic families on the Brazos River. Upon Austin's death, his son Stephen inherited the contract. The *Mapa de los Estados Unidos de Mejico* (above) was produced in 1828. The Colorado and Red River Land Company created a map in 1832 to mark Austin's colony. (Both courtesy Texas State Library and Archives Commission.)

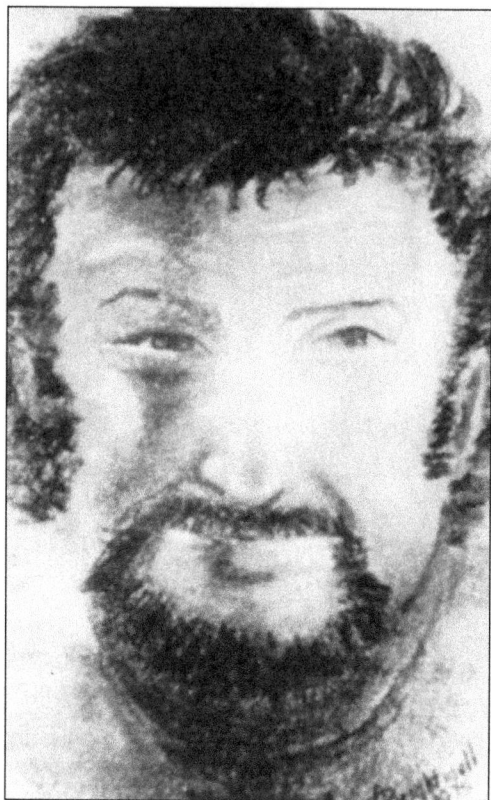

Aylette C. "Strap" Buckner (left), a red-headed giant of a man, settled in Fayette County in 1821–1822 before Stephen F. Austin (below) began to colonize the area. He and Austin began a violent quarrel when Austin refused to grant Buckner the land he desired. The two managed to settle their differences, however, in order to deal with Native American deprivations. Strap was known for his strength. It is said that he would innocently thump a man on the back so hard he would go reeling to the ground. Legend has it that a big, black bull named Noche had been terrorizing the settlers until Strap hit him with his fist, sending the bull fleeing. In 1832, Buckner lost his life at the Battle of Velasco. (Below courtesy Texas State Library and Archives Commission.)

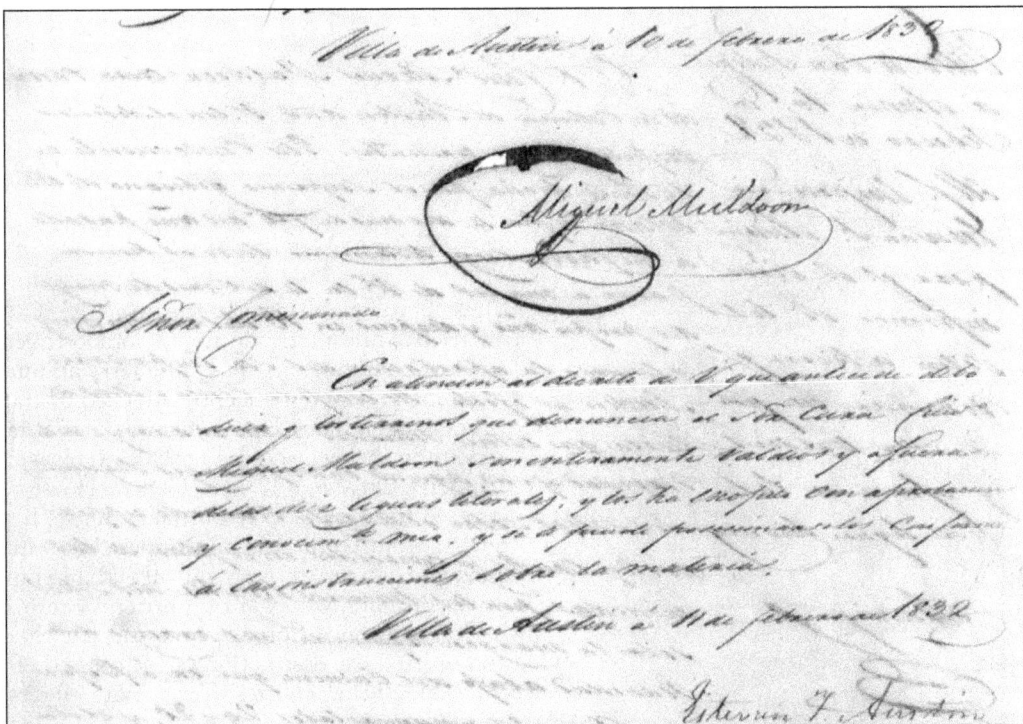

Educated in Spain, Irish priest Miguel Muldoon came to Mexico in 1821. From 1831 to 1832, he tended to the spiritual needs of Protestants living in the La Grange area. He supplied Catholic baptismal and marriage certificates and converted citizens to Catholicism so they could own land. Soon these individuals were cynically known as "Muldoon Catholics." In return, Stephen F. Austin paid the priest with 11 leagues of land in the area. (Above courtesy Texas General Land Office; right courtesy FPLMA.)

Jesse Burnam (left), one of Austin's "Old 300" settlers, built a ferry on the Colorado River below La Grange in 1824. The ferry and its trading post were frequently attacked by the Kawakawa Indians. However, it was Gen. Sam Houston (below) who dealt the death blow to the ferry. On March 17, 1836, General Houston crossed the Colorado at Burnam's during his retreat from Gen. Antonio López de Santa Anna and ordered the ferry and all outbuildings burned. Burnam, who was on unfriendly terms with Houston, never forgave him and felt that Houston ordered the destruction out of spite. (Left courtesy FPLMA; below courtesy Texas State Library and Archives Commission.)

In 1828, John Henry Moore built a twin blockhouse as a defense against the Native Americans. Called Moore's Fort, it was located at the present site of La Grange. He fought vigorously against the Native Americans, led the Red Fork Massacre (below), and commanded the Texians at Gonzales in 1835. Moore is thought to have designed the "Come and Take It" banner, taunting the Mexicans to take the cannon the Texians held. He was a challenging man. He is widely believed to have planned the shooting death of one of his sons-in-law and, upon his own death, left no money to his daughter Tabitha or her family. Moore died in 1880. (Right courtesy FPLMA.)

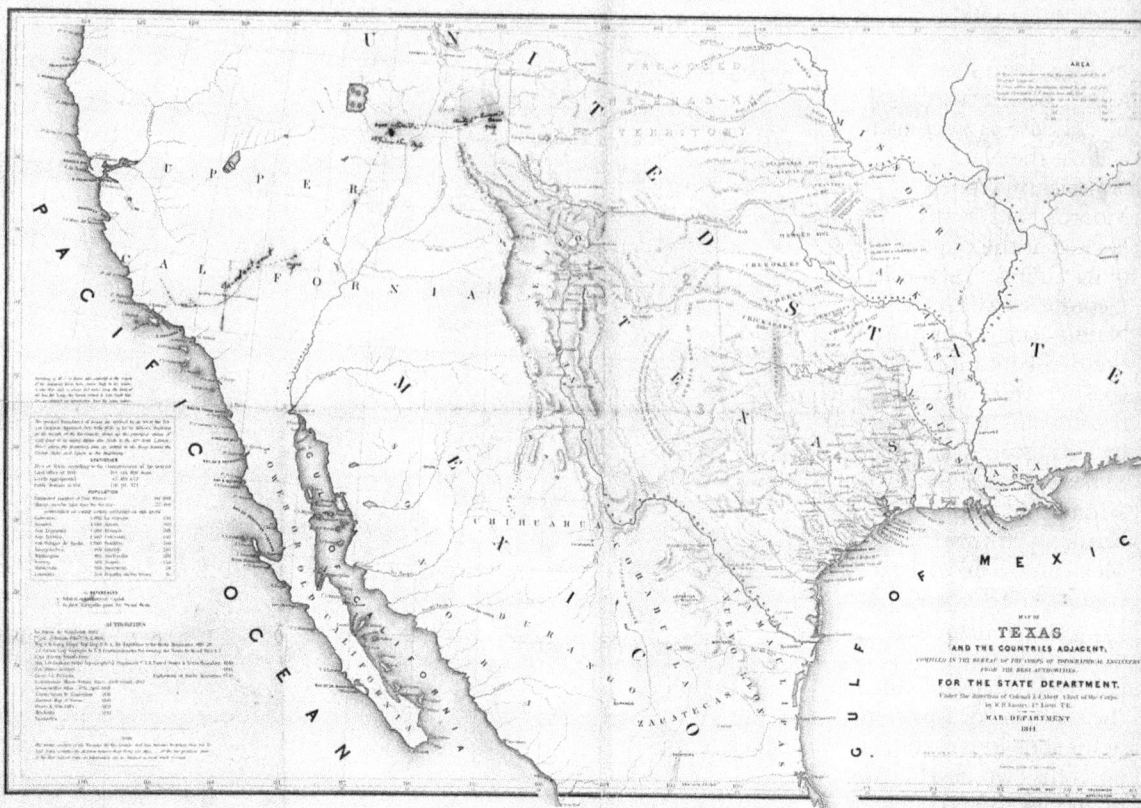

By the fall of 1835, Anglo colonists and Tejanos were becoming increasingly concerned about Santa Anna's dictatorship, which destroyed freedoms established in the Constitution of 1824. T. Archer, William H. Whorton, and Stephen F. Austin headed to the United States to raise money for the cause while a delegation met at Washington-on-the-Brazos. Of the 59 who attended the convention, two were native Tejanos, one was born in Mexico, and only 10 had been in Texas by 1836. The rest were mainly from the United States and Europe. On March 2, 1836, the delegates signed a declaration of independence and, on March 16, produced a governmental structure modeled after the United States; legalized slavery prevented free blacks from living in Texas without permission from Congress and did not allow ministers of the gospel to hold office. Sam Houston was elected commander of the army and went to take control at Gonzalez. Upon hearing of the defeat at the Alamo, he retreated through Burnam's crossing all the way to San Jacinto, where he miraculously beat Santa Anna in a decisive battle that lasted only 18 minutes. This map of Texas and the adjacent countries was published in 1844. (Courtesy Texas State Library and Archives Commission.)

Houston was named temporary capital of the republic while a search for a permanent location commenced. Committee members from the House and Senate met at Moore's plantation and secured a contract with John Eblin, whose land bordered Moore's, to purchase his league of land for the permanent capital. On May 9, 1838, a joint congressional session voted overwhelmingly to make Eblin League the capital with the following provisions: that it be named Austin, that one square mile be set aside as a university, and that the capital remain in Houston until 1840. Sam Houston vetoed the bill, infuriating La Grange citizens. The results of the congressional vote are recorded in the 1838 *Journal of the House of Representatives of the Republic of Texas.* (Both courtesy Texas State Library and Archives Commission.)

The senate, conducted by their president, were received into the hall, and the purpose for which the two houses had met having been explained by the speaker, they proceeded, by joint vote, to select a site for the permanent location of the seat of government. The following places were put in nomination:

Mr. Robertson nominated Nashville;
Mr. Sutherland nominated Eblin's league;
Mr. Burleson nominated Bastrop;
Mr. Wilson nominated Black's place;
Mr. Jones, of Austin, nominated San Felipe de Austin;
Mr. Boyd nominated Nacogdoches;
Mr. Wilson nominated Groce's Retreat;
Mr. Everett nominated Comanchie;
Mr. Jones, of Brazoria, nominated the city of Richmond.

The vote was then taken as follows:
For Nashville—Messrs. Pierpont, Walker and Robertson.—3.

For Eblin's league—Messrs. Speaker, Baker, Brennan, Grigsby, Hardeman, Linn, Lumpkin, Menifee, Patton, Ponton, Power, Sutherland, Thornton, Wyatt and —— —19.

For Bastrop—Messrs. Burleson, Billingsly, Gazley, and McKinny—4.

For Black's place—Messrs. Branch, Rusk, Rowlett, Thompson and —— —5.

For San Felipe de Austin—Messrs. Jones, of Austin, and —— —2.

For Nacogdoches—Messrs. Douglass, Swift, and —— —5.

Groce's Retreat—none.

For Comanchie—Messrs. Boyd and —— —2.

For the Mound league—Messrs. Hill, and Jones, of Brazoria —2.

For the city of Richmond—none.

Mr. Gant voted for Washington.

No place having received a majority, the vote was again taken, (Camanchie was withdrawn.)

For Nashville—Mr. —— —1.

For Eblin's league—Messrs. Speaker, Burleson, Billingsly, Brennan, Gazley, Grigsby, Hardeman, Hill, Jones, of Brazoria, Linn, Lumpkin, Menifee, McKinny, Patton, Ponton, Power, Sutherland, Swift, Thornton, Wyatt, and —— —27.

98

For Bastrop—Mr. Boyd.
For Black's place—Messrs. Branch, Douglass, Pierpont, Rusk, Rowlett, Thompson, Walker and —— —10.
For San Felipe de Austin—none.
For Nacogdoches—none.
For Groce's Retreat—none.
For the Mound league—Messrs. Jones, of Austin, and —— —2.
For the city of Richmond—none.
Mr. Gant voted for Washington, and Mr. Baker voted for Bexar.
Eblin's league received a majority of all the votes.
The senate then withdrew.

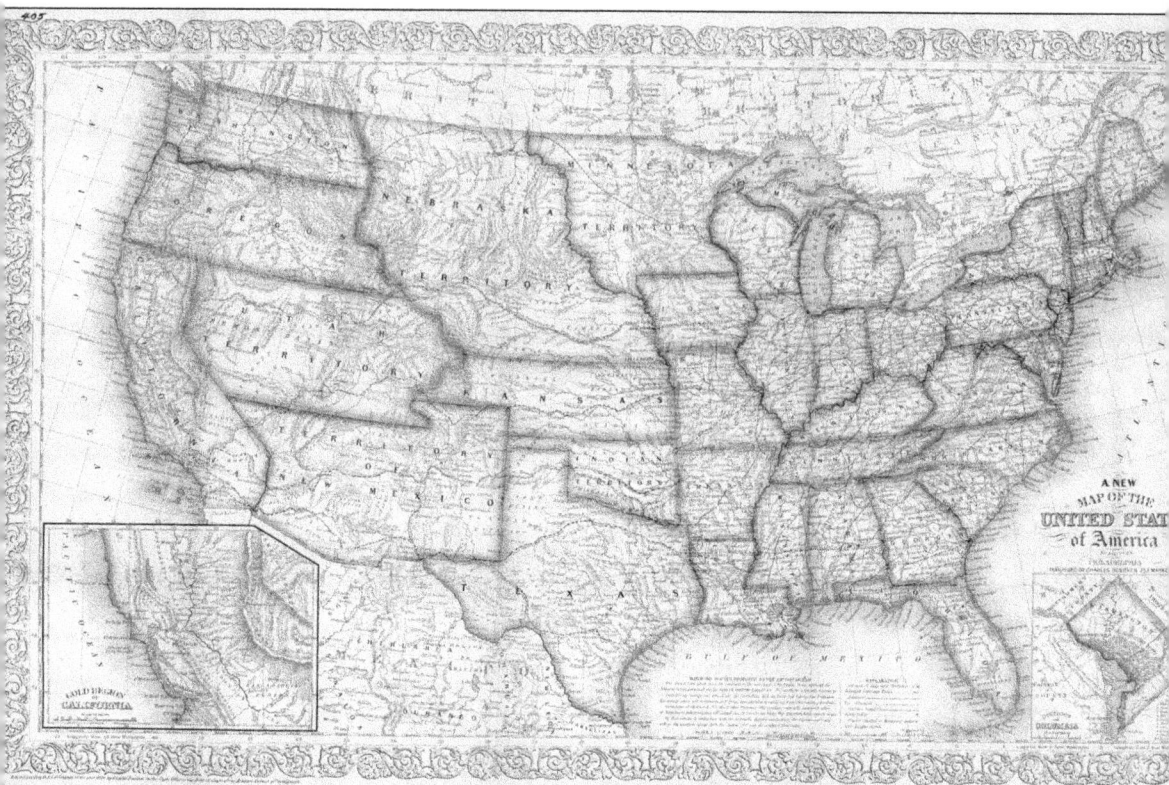

Becoming a part of the United States was a feat that took Texas nearly 10 years to accomplish. In 1836, the Van Buren administration turned Texas down over fear of a war with Mexico. By 1842, Texas was again being threatened by Mexico, which wanted to regain control of its rebellious territory. Fearing Texas could not be protected, Houston proposed annexation during his second term as president (1841–1844), to no avail. It was Great Britain's meddling that did the trick. Afraid Texas would become a satellite of Great Britain, the U.S. Congress passed an annexation resolution on February 28, 1845, and Texas formally entered the United States on December 29, 1845. This new map of the United States was published in 1856. (Courtesy Texas State Library and Archives Commission.)

As talk of trouble between North and South grew, Unionist sentiment in Fayette Country became strong. However, when Lincoln was elected president, a black flag was run up the flagpole on the square as a sign of mourning. On February 23, 1861, the voters of Fayette County went to the polls to determine whether Texas should secede from the Union. After a total of 1,206 votes were cast, the anti-secessionists won by a margin of 46 votes. Most of the county, however, supported the Confederacy by serving or contributing to the cause. (Right courtesy Texas State Library and Archives Commission.)

To the Secretary of State :

Returns of an Election held in the County of _Fayette_ on the 23d day of February A. D. 1861, pursuant to Laws, and the Proclamation of the Governor of the State of Texas, at which the question of "Secession" from the United States was voted upon by the qualified electors of the State.

	NO. OF VOTES		NO. OF VOTES
For Secession.	580	Against Secession.	626

I, _____, Chief Justice of the County aforesaid, do hereby certify that the above and foregoing is a true and correct Return of said Election, as appears by the returns of the same made to me by the Managers of said Election in and for said County.

Given under my hand, and the Seal of the County Court, at __La Grange__ this the __twenty sixth__ day of __February__ A. D. 1861.

(TX)

Chief Justice _Fayette_ County.

Returns required by Law to be made on or before the 26th day of February, 1861.

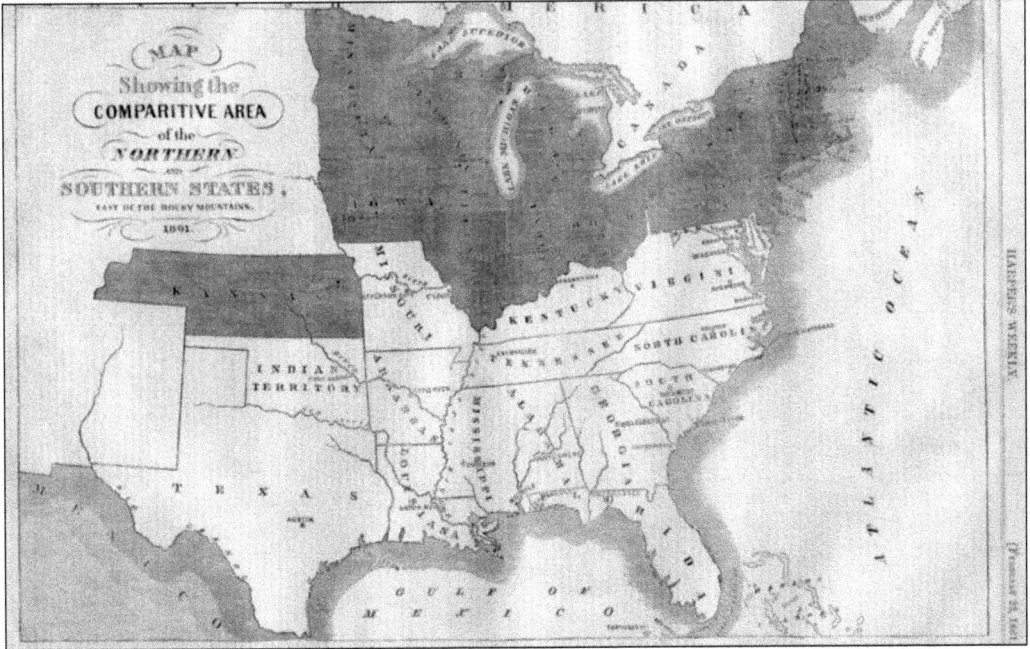

MAP Showing the COMPARITIVE AREA of the NORTHERN AND SOUTHERN STATES, EAST OF THE ROCKY MOUNTAINS. 1861.

Although not a national banner, the *Frisch Auf!* flag deserves a place as one of the flags flying over La Grange. As early as 1831, German-born immigrants began to settle in Texas, mostly between the Brazos and Colorado Rivers, an area that became known as Kleindeutschland. By the 1840s, German immigrant Heinrich Kreische had settled on the bluff above La Grange and eventually became a brewer of German-style lager. Legend says that the *Frisch Auf!* ("Freshen Up!") flag was raised on the bluff overlooking La Grange to let residents know that beer was ready for sale at the Kreische Brewery. Below, the flag waves at Kreische's pavilion on the bluff. (Both courtesy Monument Hill and Kreische Brewery State Historic Site.)

Two

Always Ready for a Good Fight

La Grange residents have never been shy about stepping up and fighting for their beliefs. During the colonization of Texas and the era of the Republic of Texas, all soldiers were citizen soldiers. The need for manpower was critical. In 1837, the Congress of the Republic of Texas passed a supplemental militia act that accepted able-bodied males over 17 and less than 50 years of age. It also required young men turning 17 or men new to a district to enroll in a militia company in their county. Each man had to provide his own equipment, including a good musket, a suitable bayonet, belt, six flints, knapsack, and cartridge box with 24 suitable ball cartridges. He had an option to carry a rifle, yager, or shotgun, but provided his own knapsack with a shot pouch, powder horn, 50 balls suitable to the caliber of this gun, and half a pound of powder.

When called, La Grange area men met under the Muster Oak on the town square and organized for battle. They frequently fought Native Americans but soon turned their attention to the Mexicans as Santa Anna chased Sam Houston all the way to southeast Texas. Approximately 50 Fayette County citizens stood and fought for independence at the Battle of San Jacinto.

Peace did not last long. In 1842, Mexican general Adrián Woll invaded San Antonio twice. During the second invasion, citizen soldiers met at the Muster Oak and rode to the rescue under the leadership of Capt. Nicholas Mosby Dawson. The group ran into a large force of Mexicans, and within about an hour, 36 were dead, 15 were taken prisoner, and 3 managed to escape. This incident is now known as the Dawson Massacre. President Houston sent Gen. Alexander Somervell to the rescue, but his force stopped at the Mexican border. Disgusted, a group of about 308 Texans disobeyed orders and continued into Mexico in what is called the Mier Expedition—again with disastrous consequences.

Despite these setbacks, La Grange citizens have never failed to answer the call to war.

Riding sidesaddle on a tall iron-gray horse named Tormenter, Mary Crownover Rabb (left) came to the La Grange area in 1823 with her husband, John, as one of Stephen F. Austin's original colonists. In 1836, while John fought with the Texians, Mary joined the Runaway Scrape. During the flight, all suffered from hunger and cold, and her three-month-old son, Lorenzo, died on the road. They returned home after Santa Anna's defeat to find everything of value either stolen or burned. Despite early hardships, the Rabbs (below) prospered and made a generous contribution of land and money to establish Rutersville College in 1840. (Courtesy FPLMA.)

Around 1822, Sylvanus Castleman and his family (including his daughter Louvenia, pictured) settled near La Grange as one of Austin's 300. Native Americans plagued the family by stealing horses and plundering the cabin. The family then adopted a policy of shooting Native Americans on sight. Sylvanus learned to scalp his enemies—dead or alive—and he and his sons reportedly used the scalps as razor strops. (Courtesy FPLMA.)

Upon hearing about the fall of the Alamo, Lucinda Gorham panicked and fled Santa Anna's approaching army during the Runaway Scrape. Her group camped the first night and, upon awakening, was surrounded by 25 Comanches, who took the horses. A vote was held (women included) to continue rather than to wait on the Texian army. The Comanches reappeared and circled the group. Men drew guns, and women waved sticks. Finally they left. (Courtesy FPLMA.)

Joel Walter Robison served his country in both war and peace. His war exploits include time as a Native American fighter under Capt. John York, the 1832 Battle of Velasco, the 1835 Siege of Bexar, the Grass Fight, and the Battle of Concepción. During the Battle of San Jacinto, he rode with the group that captured Santa Anna (who was hiding in the uniform of a private). It is said that Santa Anna entered the Texian camp riding double on Robison's horse. Robison later served as elected commissioner of the Fayette County Land Office, representative to the Eighth Legislature, member of the Constitutional Convention of 1875, and second vice president of the Texas Veterans Association. In a rendition of artist William Huddle's painting (below), Sam Houston meets Santa Anna after the Battle of San Jacinto. (Left courtesy Texas State Cemetery.)

Napoleon "Pole" and Charlotte Breeding have the first recorded marriage in Fayette County, in 1838. Despite Pole's frequent absences to fight for his beliefs, the couple managed to have six children. His list of service includes the 1835 Siege of Bexar, the Battle of San Jacinto, and the 1843 Snively Expedition. This expedition was supposed to capture spoils of Mexican traders who crossed through Texas on their way to Santa Fe. However, it met with little success. For his service at San Jacinto, where he guarded the baggage, he was given 640 acres of land. Pole died in Fayette County in 1865. (Courtesy FPLMA.)

Nicholas Mosby Dawson arrived in Velasco, Texas, aboard the schooner *Pennsylvania* on January 28, 1836, and immediately joined the Texian army. In September 1842, Dawson heard that the Mexicans had invaded San Antonio. He then met citizens under the Muster Oak and rode to the rescue. On September 18, the men quickly found themselves surrounded by Mexican soldiers near San Antonio. In the midst of the carnage, Dawson put up a white flag of surrender, but neither side ceased firing. Dawson was among those killed. A monument was erected in front of the Fayette County Courthouse in his honor. (Courtesy FPLMA.)

In 1833 at the age of 13, Edward Manton migrated to the La Grange area. He did not see military action until March 1842, when he joined Rabb's company of Fayette County volunteers and pursued Mexican general Rafael Vásquez as he retreated from San Antonio into Mexico. For this military act, Manton received 640 acres of land. Joining Dawson later that year at the Muster Oak, he became one of the 15 survivors of the Dawson Massacre to be taken prisoner and marched to Perote Prison in Mexico. His letters home describe the march he made while chained to N. W. Faison and the bleak existence at the prison. He was released on March 23, 1844. Manton, along with Faison, returned to the scene of the massacre in 1848 to gather the bones of his fallen comrades. They were later reburied on the bluff overlooking La Grange with full military honors along with the remains of those who died in the Mier Expedition. Manton continued to increase his landholdings until he died on August 20, 1893. (Courtesy Prints and Photographs Collection, CN 10815, Center for American History, University of Texas at Austin.)

Being only 5 feet 6 inches tall did not stop David Smith Kornegay from joining a good fight. He arrived in Texas in 1830, lived for a time with Col. John H. Moore, battled Native Americans in 1835, and fought at San Jacinto in 1836. For his service, Kornegay received a total of 1,060 acres of land. In 1842, he joined Dawson and other citizens at the Muster Oak. Though one of the captured, he did not stay at Perote Prison long. Along with 15 others, he tunneled out beneath the walls and, with help from the outside, managed to make it to Veracruz and then to safety. He married Elizabeth McGary in La Grange in 1844. (Courtesy Doss Kornegay.)

Kornegay married Elizabeth McGary in La Grange in 1844. Elizabeth came to Texas from Louisiana at the age of eight with her mother and three siblings via boat, participated in the Runaway Scrape, and lost a brother to the Comanches. Together she and David had five children. (Courtesy Doss Kornegay.)

Joe Griffin, a mulatto slave, traveled to San Antonio with ransom money to free his owner, Samuel Maverick, who was taken hostage by the Mexicans in 1842 while attending the fall term of the district court. Armed with a shotgun, Griffin rode a mule and carried $380. Though he was the last to join Dawson's group, he fought so ferociously that he came to the attention of Mexican cavalry colonel Jose Carraso. Out of ammunition, he used his shotgun as a club, knocking three lancers from their saddles. When the shotgun broke, Griffin continued to fight with a mesquite limb and was finally killed by the Mexicans. Colonel Carraso later reported to Maverick that he had witnessed the feats performed by that "valiant black man" and that Griffin was the bravest man he had ever seen. Here Eddie Harrison portrays Joe Griffin at the 2005 Heroes Day at Monument Hill and Kreische Brewery State Historic Site. (Courtesy author.)

**DAWSON MEN KILLED AT SALADO, TEXAS
SUNDAY SEPT. 18, 1842
CAPT. NICHOLAS MOSBY DAWSON
LIEUTENANT DICKERSON**

DAMS
B. ALEXANDER
BARCLEY
RCLEY
EARD
BERRY
1S E. BROOKFIELD
AS J. BUTLER
CHURCH
CUMMINGS

JOHN DANSER
ROBERT EASTLAND
—— FARRIS
CHARLES FIELDS
ELIJAH GAREY
JOE GRIFFIN (c)
HARVEY HALL
GEORGE HILL
ASA JONES
WILLIAM LINN
—— THREE NAMES MISSING ——

RICHARD McGEE
JOHN WESLEY PENDLETO
THOMAS RICE
WILLIAM SAVAGE
ELAM SCALLORN
JOHN WESLEY SCALLORN
THOMAS SIMMS
JOHN SLACK
NED. TRIMBLE
ZADOCK WOODS

Old 300 settler Zadock Woods was the eldest of the Dawson party members and a veteran of just about every military action since 1823. Family legend states that his family tried to keep him from going to the aid of San Antonio in September 1842 but that he mounted his favorite mare and, with long rifle in hand, circled his house reciting how the Mexicans had tried to get him before and they were going to get another chance. The Dawson group voted to join the Battle of Salado Creek after Woods said, "We have marched a long way to meet the Mexicans, and I do not intend to return without meeting them. I had rather die than retreat." Woods died in battle on his 80th birthday. The names of those who lost their lives during the Dawson Massacre are engraved on the tomb at Monument Hill and Kreische Brewery State Historic Site. (Courtesy author.)

Gold fever did to John Murchison what Native American arrows and an assassin's bullets could not. In 1838, he participated in the Battle of Kickapoo, during which some 700 Texians were attacked by about 900 Mexicans and Native Americans. The Texians prevailed, and Murchison eventually recovered from his severe wounds. A man who had a grudge against Murchison shot at him twice: the first time, the bullet hit his baby daughter, wounding her in the arm; the next, the bullet passed through Murchison's chest. Eventually, Murchison organized a party of 100 men to find fortune in California. On July 28, 1849, he died in California when his gun accidentally discharged. (Courtesy FPLMA.)

Jon Winfield Scott Dancy was not only a fighter but an innovator. He came to Texas in 1836 and immediately fought the Native Americans with Colonel Moore. In the U.S. war against Mexico, he served as a private in a spy company of Texas mounted volunteers and as a colonel under his cousin Gen. Winfield Scott. Dancy served in the Republic of Texas Congress, the State of Texas Senate, and as a delegate to the Secessionist Convention. He also introduced long-staple cotton to Texas, developed Texas's first hydraulic ram to provide irrigation for his plantation, participated in the founding of Rutersville College, and advocated for railroads, earning him the nickname "Father of Texas Railroads." (Courtesy Lennie Brown.)

When Gen. Alexander Somervell ordered Texas troops home on December 19, 1842, some 308 rebellious citizen soldiers disobeyed, determined to seek revenge for the Mexican invasions of Texas. The group, under the command of Capt. William S. Fisher, attacked the Mexican town of Mier on Christmas Day. After fierce fighting, the men surrendered and were marched into the interior of Mexico, where they would be incarcerated at Perote Prison. On February 11, 1843, some 188 Texians made a break at Rancho Salado, about 200 miles from the Rio Grande. The escape was a disaster, and 176 men were recaptured; only 5 reached Texas. Furious, Santa Anna ordered the prisoners put to death. After protests erupted, Santa Anna backed off, requiring that only one in 10 be executed. The men were forced to draw a bean from a pot—white meant life, while black meant death. Those 17 men who drew the black bean were allowed to write home and then were bound together and shot.

In 1834, William Mosby Eastland moved to Texas with his family and settled in the La Grange area. Soon he was busy fighting the Native Americans. At the Battle of San Jacinto, during which he served as first lieutenant, it is said his response to Sam Houston's orders to stop killing Mexican fugitives and take them prisoner was, "Boys take prisners, you know how to take prisners, take them with the but of guns, club guns, & said remember the Alamo remember Laberde [La Bahía], & club guns, right & left, & nock there brains out." Eager for revenge of the death of his cousin Nicolas Mosby Dawson, Eastland joined the Mier group in 1842. Eastland was the first Texan to draw a black bean and the only officer to do so. He was executed on March 25, 1843, after sending word to his wife that "I die in the faith in which I have lived."

At the age of 14, John Christopher Columbus Hill (left) accompanied his father and brother on the 1842 Mier Expedition. During the battle, his bravery caught the attention of Mexican general Pedro Ampudia, who sent him to Pres. Santa Anna (below left) in Mexico City. After he agreed to be adopted by Santa Anna, his brother and father were released from prison. During the U.S. occupation of Mexico City in the Mexican War, Hill served as an interpreter, aiding both sides. He had a full career in Mexico as a civil engineer, mining engineer, and practicing physician. Although he made frequent trips to the United States to visit his family, he married a Mexican woman and spent most of his life there. After the death of his first wife, he married his childhood sweetheart, Mary Ann Murray Masterson, a native of England. On February 16, 1904, Hill died in Monterrey, Nuevo León, where he is also buried. (Bottom courtesy Library of Congress.)

John Rufus Alexander moved to Texas too late to fight for independence, but he was eager to get into battle. He joined the Somervell Expedition and, refusing to turn back at the border, crossed into Mexico to meet Captain Fisher at the Battle of Mier. After 18 hours of combat, the men surrendered and, bound together, began their march to Perote Prison. Alexander escaped and, along with William S. Oldham, arrived in San Antonio after 600 miles of tortuous travel. After recovering, he moved to the La Grange area and married Mary Fisher Jones, with whom he had 11 children. Still itching for a fight, he joined the La Grange Company called the Dixie Greys during the Civil War because he said he could still drop a "Damyankee" at 60 yards. The last surviving member of the Mier Expedition, he died in 1908. (Courtesy FPLMA.)

The 4th Texas Confederate Calvary Company G was organized in 1861 and boasted many La Grange citizens. These soldiers, like two-thirds of Texans who served in the war, preferred the cavalry. Lt. Col. Arthur Femantle of the British Coldstream Guards visited Texas during the war, noting that it was hard to raise infantry because "no Texan walks a yard if he can help it." Pictured here are surviving veterans. (Courtesy FPLMA.)

Approximately 800 area men either joined the Confederate army or were conscripted. Many active and reserve companies formed in the county, including Capt. Louis Strobel's Company F, which joined Terry's Rangers in 1861. A Ranger reunion is shown here.

Not all La Grange citizens were ready for a good fight. A number of German men evaded conscription, and in January 1863, a committee of Germans met with Gen. W. G. Webb in La Grange and presented a written statement of grievances and unwillingness to defend the state. Upon notification of the meeting, Gen. John Magruder (right) dispatched soldiers with a piece of artillery to La Grange, declared martial law in three counties, and had the ringleaders arrested. Gov. Francis Richard Lubbock (below) held a conference with the disgruntled group, which resulted in the enrollment of some of the drafted men. (Courtesy Library of Congress.)

At least 40 Fayette County residents did manage to escape the draft. While they were headed to Mexico, a military committee of 10 overtook them and ordered them to return. The draft evaders told the conscript officers to go home and keep quiet or they would be put where no secrets are told. The conscript officers left peacefully. (Courtesy Texas State Library and Archives Commission.)

The Civil War strained family relationships, particularly for the Lidiak family. Joseph Lidiak (shown at left) left Moravia and settled in Hostyn, just outside La Grange, in 1860. In this bohemian settlement, he farmed until joining the Confederate army as a corporal in 1863. His son John (below) hauled cotton to Brownsville for a neighbor. When returning, he met friends who persuaded him to enlist in the Union army. Unaware that his father had joined the Confederacy, he enlisted in Hammet's Company. Both survived and returned to live together on the farm. The cannons located on the Queen of the Holy Rosary Parish grounds in Hostyn are dedicated in their honor. (Both courtesy FPLMA.)

"How many broken hearts this war will make," Ellen Porter Phelps mused in her diary. Originally from Illinois, she taught school in the La Grange area. She recorded rumors and reports about the progress of the Civil War, feared Galveston would be invaded, listened to political debates, and discussed battles with the men. When not writing about the war, she mentioned visits with friends for tea and bemoaned the fact that Northern papers and letters were not allowed into the county. The sewing club, she reported, was making tents and uniforms while many were knitting socks. While she recorded the seemingly mundane happenings around her, she realized that what was occurring in the country would change it forever. (Courtesy FPLMA.)

Yankee blockades meant La Grange residents could not acquire products such as cloth and thread. By 1862, Jon Dancy realized he would need to produce textiles, so he set up 12 spinning wheels and a loom. His daughter Martha Evelina "Lena" Dancy became fascinated with the process of making cloth. In 1864 at the age of 14, she created her own dress, displayed here on a too-tall model in 1918. In a time of scarcity, Lena had a gorgeous dress that would have been the envy of Northern and Southern women alike. (Courtesy Ledbetter [Lena Dancy] Papers, 1830–1950, CN 06266, Center for American History, University of Texas at Austin.)

Sgt. Hugo J. Ehlers was one in a long line of La Grange citizens to fight for what he believed. He was a member of the 143rd Infantry, 36th Division, of the American Expeditionary Force during World War I. The 36th Infantry Division was comprised mostly of Texas National Guardsmen, who arrived at their rendezvous with destiny with meager equipment, depleted ranks, and high morale. The only La Grange resident to lose his life in battle during World War I, Sergeant Ehlers was killed near Suippes and Somme-Suippes, France, on October 10, 1918, as the 143rd worked to clean out a small system of trenches the Germans held near Suippes and Somme-Suippes, France. On November 11, 1918, an armistice was signed ending hostilities and Ehlers's parents were notified of his death the next day. His funeral was held at the Presbyterian church on September 30, 1920, where he was given a hero's farewell. (Courtesy FPLMA.)

Three

WILLING AND UNWILLING IMMIGRANTS

Settlers from the United States were not the only ones drawn to La Grange. The majority of African Americans who came to the area were brought as slaves to assist in the production of corn, tobacco, wool, and cotton. On the eve of the Civil War, Fayette County was home to 3,786 slaves out of a total county population of 11,604. After the war, many African Americans worked as sharecroppers on the way to becoming self-sufficient free men and women. By 1900, about 33 percent of the county's inhabitants were black. That number would drop to 10 percent by 2000.

German immigrant Johann Friedrich Ernst received 4,000 acres in nearby Austin County in 1831 and soon began to write home of mild winters; abundant game and fish; rich, fertile soil; low taxes; and cheap land. While stressing the positives, he forgot to mention the negatives. Before long, one of his letters appeared in a German newspaper and guidebook. Neighbors told other neighbors, and soon Germans began immigrating to Texas. Most were middle-class peasants who believed their futures were stymied by the social and economic system at home. The German culture and language flourished in the area but began to decline with acculturation and the unpopularity of Germany during World Wars I and II.

Czech immigrants from Moravia and Bohemia also began to flock to Texas as a result of letter writing. Rev. Josef Arnošt Bergmann arrived in Austin County in 1850 and started writing his friends about the opportunities to escape political and religious oppression, conscription in the military of the Austrian Empire, and poor economic conditions. Like the Germans, the Czechs still take pride in their traditional language, music, dancing, and foods.

Today a new immigrant has arrived in La Grange, adding to the diverse ethnic background of the region. Latinos only make up approximately 13 percent of the population of Fayette County but account for 26 percent of the students in the La Grange Independent School District.

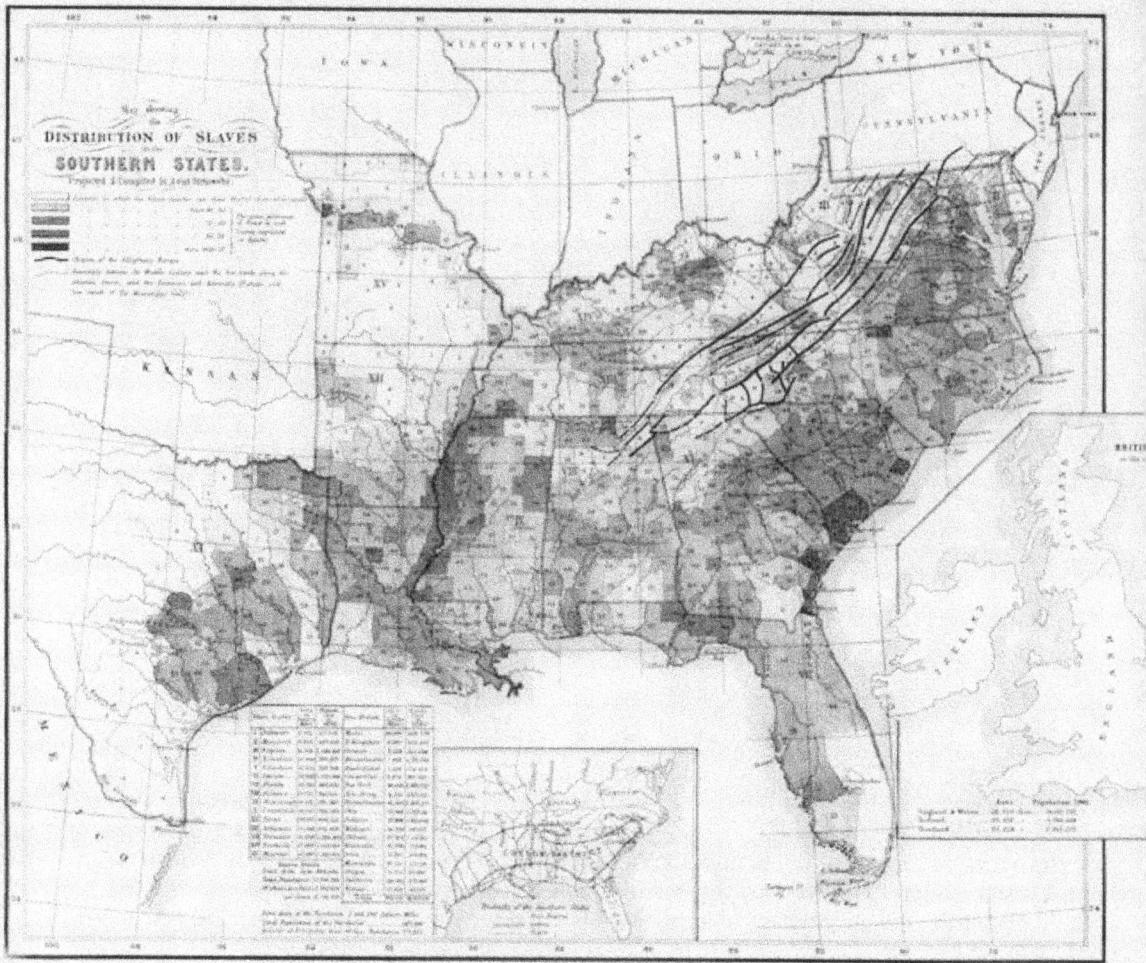

African Americans were among the earliest settlers of Texas. By 1792, Spanish Texas numbered 34 blacks and 414 mulattos. Some of them were free men and women. Most blacks, however, entered the state as slaves. During Mexican rule, slavery was illegal. With Texas independence, though, the slave population grew rapidly. Fayette County's slave population was 206 in 1840. By 1850, it had increased to 820, and by 1855, the number had reached 2,072. While some slaves were treated well (like Joe Griffin), others received harsh treatment. Although slavery ended with the conclusion of the Civil War, African Americans continued to be treated as second-class citizens, subjected to racial prejudice and denied the basic human rights others took for granted. (Courtesy Library of Congress.)

On the eve of the Civil War, high prices were paid for slaves in La Grange. On February 5, 1859, the newspaper *True Issue* boasted, "A negro girl, 18 years of age, was sold at the Court-house door on last Tuesday, and knocked off at $1161 cash. The country is in a flourishing condition when property commands such prices." These two notices were printed in the 1844 *La Grange Intelligencer*. One threatens slaves who have no pass from their master with 100 lashes, while the other announces the sale of a slave to satisfy his owner's debts. (Both courtesy Texas State Library and Archives Commission.)

On June 19, 1865, Union general Gordon Granger (left) read General Order No. 3 to the public in Galveston, Texas: "The people are informed that in accordance with a Proclamation from the Executive of the United States, all slaves are free. . . . The freed are advised to remain at their present homes, and work for wages. They are informed that they will not be allowed to collect at military posts; and that they will not be supported in idleness either there or elsewhere." As early as 1870, Juneteenth was celebrated in La Grange. A parade is shown below. (Left courtesy Library of Congress; below courtesy Jeff Kelly.)

in favor of V. Srubar.

We the undersigned colored citizens of the town of LaGrange, deeply sympathizing with our fellow-townsman, Mr. J. F. McClatchy, in his recent disaster, and being anxious and willing to help him in repairing his great loss, and, having no money to give, hereby tender to him the number of days of labor, set opposite our names, said labor to be performed in building him a new stable, or upon any other work connected therewith as he may direct: Johnson Miller, six days; Reuben Pierce, six days; Jack Blocker, two days; W. A. Schropshire, two days; Granderson Lindsay, three days; Sam Rodgers, one day; George Holmes, his team one day; Urias Foster, one day; Nathan Powel, two days; Bob Lyles, one day; Richard Smith, one day.

SCHOOL.—The examination exer-

While relationships between blacks and whites in La Grange could be contentious, citizens were able to work together when disaster threatened. In May 1883, a fire broke out late at night in the rear of J. F. McClatchy's livery stable, located on the east side of the square. The blaze nearly engulfed that entire side of the square but was contained by the hard work of both black and white citizens. McClatchy, a white man from Mississippi, lost 23 horses and nearly all of his buggies. Black citizens, having no money to give, pledged labor to help him build a new stable. Their pledge is shown in this notice in a May 1883 issue of the *La Grange Journal*. (Courtesy FPLMA.)

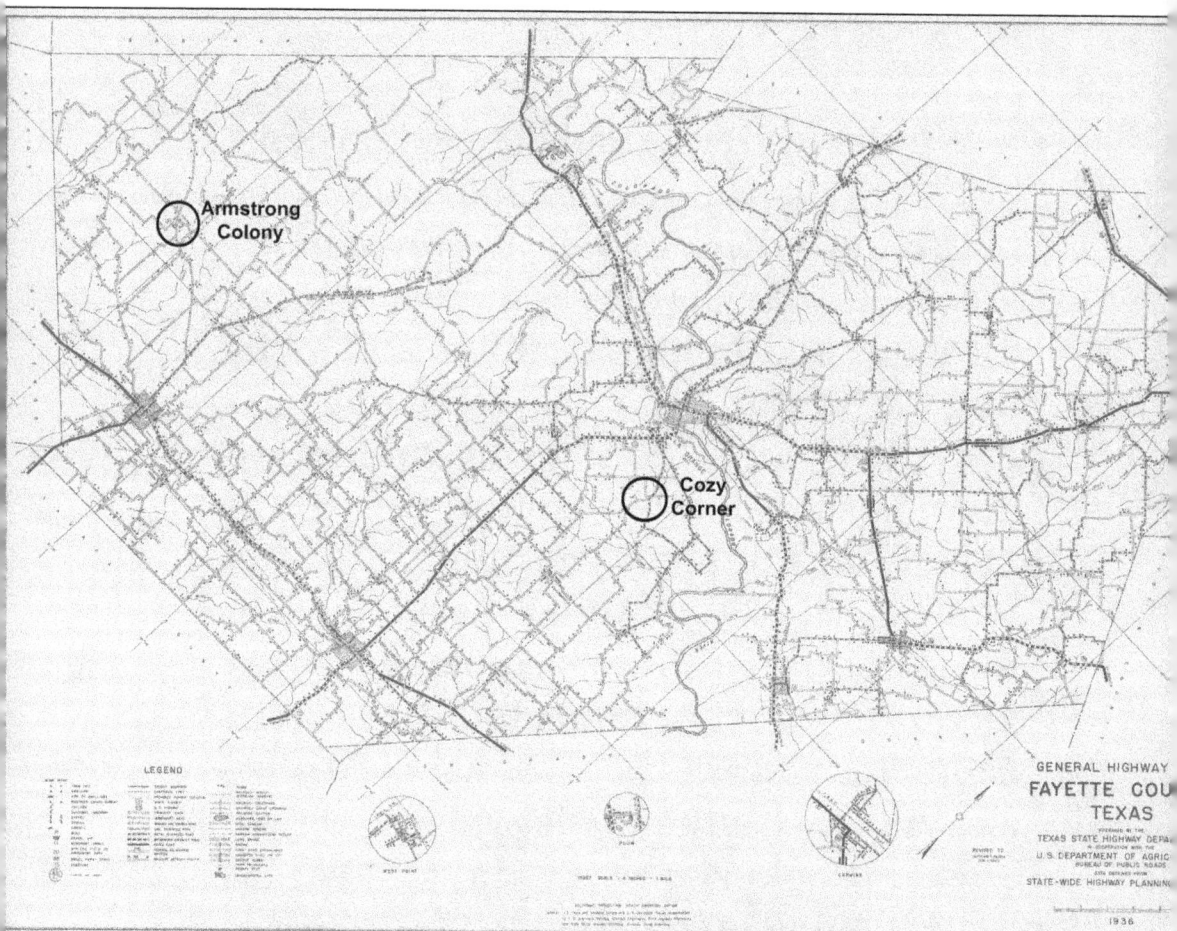

Some African Americans in Fayette County managed to avoid many of the effects of racial prejudice by forming what are now called freedom colonies. Two existed in the county: Armstrong Colony and Cozy Corner. The communities became self-sufficient and kept to themselves. Ethel Derry, who grew up in Armstrong Colony in the early 1900s, explained that her father owned land and ran a cotton gin as well as a broom factory. During her childhood, she went to town only once a year to buy shoes. This 1940 map of Fayette County identifies the freedom colonies. (Courtesy FPLMA.)

MR T. RICE AS JIM CROW.

Jim Crow was alive and well in La Grange, just like the rest of the South. The term *Jim Crow*, which was used to designate laws requiring racial segregation, was borrowed from a racially stereotyped black character in a common 19th-century song-and-dance act. Blacks were permitted only in the balcony of La Grange's Cozy Theater. Old-timers recall a basement café on the southeast corner of the square as one of the few places blacks could congregate downtown. Known by some as "the Hole" because blacks could be seen descending underground, it probably operated between 1929 and 1947. These laws were prohibited in 1964. (Courtesy Library of Congress.)

Along with Jim Crow came segregated schools. Blacks worked hard to ensure their children obtained the best possible education. G. A. Randolph (left), who had graduated from Prairie View State Normal and Industrial College with a bachelor of arts degree, came to La Grange in 1910 to run the La Grange Colored High School and provide as equal an opportunity as possible for his pupils. Professor Randolph, as he was affectionately known by his students, retired in 1941. Upon his death in 1945, the school was renamed Randolph High School in his honor. It closed in the 1960s when segregation was outlawed. (Both courtesy Jeff Kelly.)

The *Adelsverein*, also known as the *Verein zum Schutze deutscher Einwanderer in Texas* (Society for the Protection of German Immigrants in Texas), was formed by a group of German noblemen for both economic and philanthropic purposes. Between 1844 and 1846, the organization brought 7,000 German immigrants to Texas, intending to settle them on a vast tract of land known as the Fisher-Miller Grant. By 1850, one-fifth of the white population in Texas was comprised of Germans who sought a better way of life. To the right is the symbol used by the *Verein*. The map below, produced about 1845, shows the areas in Germany from which the *Verein* drew most of its immigrants around that time. (Courtesy German-Texan Heritage Society.)

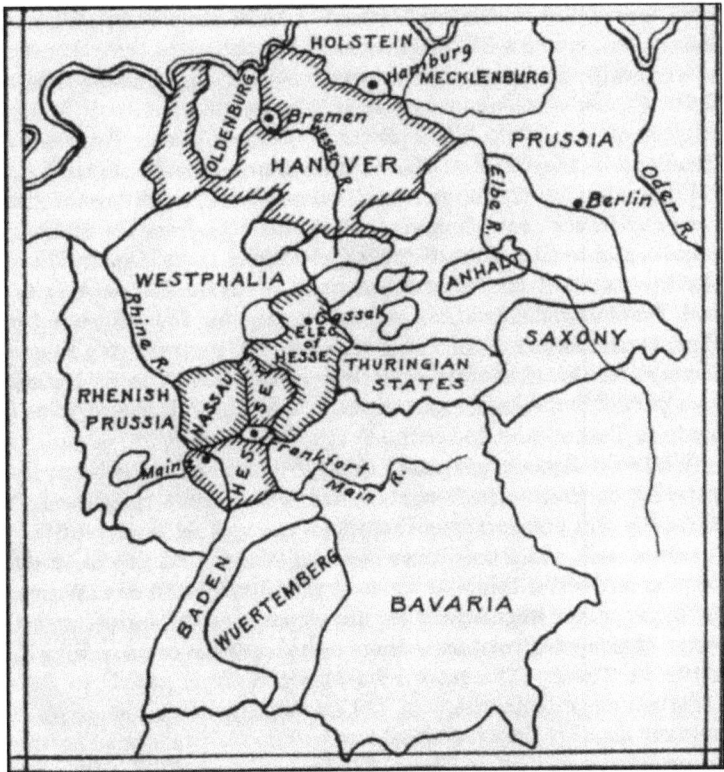

Heinrich L. Kreische, born on May 14, 1821, traveled from Saxony to Galveston, Texas, with his brother in 1846. Despite the fact that he had a certificate for two sections of land in the Fisher-Miller Grant, in 1849, he bought 172 acres on the bluff overlooking La Grange from Georg Willrich where the remains of the Mier and Dawson men had been buried the year before. He married Josepha Appelt and had six children. Unlike most residents of Fayette County, Kreische survived the Civil War with his finances intact. Between 1860 and 1870, he built a brewery on his property and settled into the business of beer. His second career flourished as he opened the Schuetzen Pavilion on the bluff and the Union Beer Hall in town. Kreische died on March 17, 1882, apparently crushed by a wagonload of stone. (Both courtesy FPLMA.)

At the brewery, Heinrich Kreische used gravity and water to his benefit. By building the three-story structure with several intermediate levels and terraces at the bottom of a ravine, he was able employ the running water for brewing, for cleaning, and for airing cool the beer via evaporation through ventilation shafts. By 1879, he was the third largest producer of beer in Texas. Kreische attracted customers with the slogans "Bluff Beer Is Good" and *Frisch Auf!* Because of a lack of pasteurization and refrigeration, his product was sold only within a 150-mile radius. His death and the coming of the railroads led to the brewery's closing. Pictured here are the brewery ruins and house. (Both courtesy Monument Hill and Kreische Brewery State Historic Site.)

In 1858, local Germans organized the Casino Association of La Grange for mutual protection and to further social and educational interests. (There is no evidence to indicate that the Casino Association sponsored gambling.) On New Year's Eve in 1881, this building was dedicated. The German cultural school occupied the first floor, while the second floor hosted social gatherings. In 1885, the City of La Grange bought the building and used it as a school until 1925. (Courtesy FPLMA.)

German immigrants brought the tradition of shooting clubs from their homeland. Such clubs originated in Germany in the 1300s and 1400s to foster marksmanship with the crossbow in order to defend cities from invaders. Local Germans established a shooting club in La Grange known as Kreische's Scheutzenverein, seen here. Kreische's son Otto appears fourth from the left in the first row. (Courtesy Monument Hill and Kreische Brewery State Historic Site.)

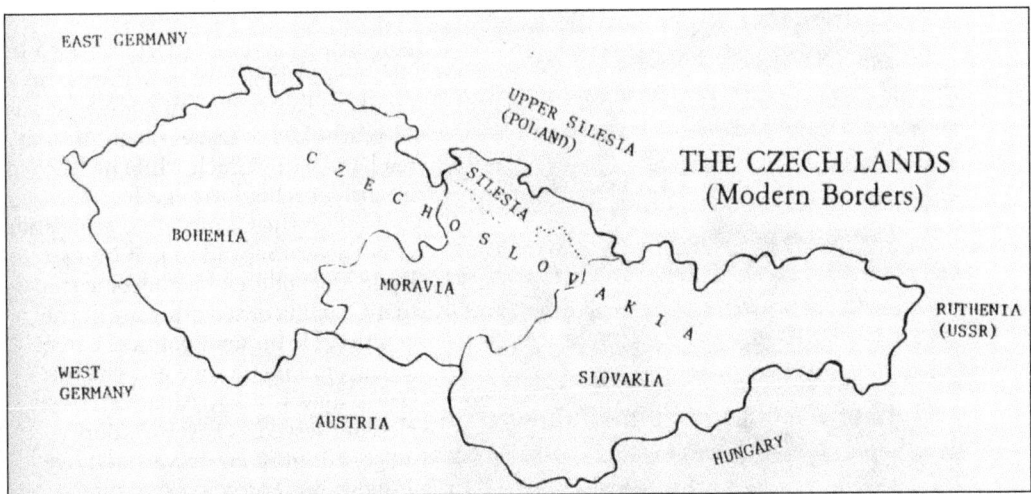

THE CZECH LANDS
(Modern Borders)

Czechs, who spoke their native language at home and were referred to as "foreign white stock" by the U.S. Census Bureau, were a Slavic people who emigrated from Bohemia, Moravia, and parts of Silesia (see map above). From the 1850s until World War I, as the Czechs spread across Texas, Fayette County was established as the center of the state's Czech population. Families were extremely close and operated as largely self-contained economic and social units. Today their luscious food such as sausage, noodles, and kolaches are area favorites. Many still enjoy polka masses and dancing to the polka beat. One of the well-known Czech bands, the Ray Baca Orchestra, is pictured below. (Below courtesy FPLMA.)

RAY BACA ORCHESTRA 1966
Left to Right: Eamil Baca, Ray Baca (Leader), Emil Hrachovy, John Simbera, Donald Cernosek, Henry Hrachovy.

Augustine Haidusek (left) was born in Moravia in 1845 and moved with his family to Fayette County when he was 11 years old. His father taught him to read and write Czech while he learned English at school. At age 16, he enlisted in the Confederate army and after the war moved to La Grange. By 1870, Haidusek had become the first Czech licensed attorney in the country. He began a political career as mayor of La Grange and the first Czech mayor of any American city. He later served as Fayette County judge. His most controversial move as judge was enforcing the state law that required English as the practical language in the classroom. When his actions angered his fellow Czechs, Haidusek started the Czech-language newspaper *Svoboda* (below) to publicize his point of view. He remained editor for more than 35 years. (Both courtesy FPLMA.)

The hardships of the Joseph Janda family illustrate the sacrifices immigrants made in order to ensure a better life for themselves and their offspring. Joseph and his wife, Anna, arrived in Galveston from Moravia in 1856 after more than three months aboard ship, during which they lost a child. They settled on the bluff just outside of La Grange and, by 1860, had bought 10 acres of land on which they farmed and built a crude log cabin. Two more children succumbed to yellow fever in 1864. In 1866, while Janda was hunting wild hogs, he missed his shot and the angered hogs attacked his dog. He swung his rifle at a hog but his gun discharged, shooting Janda in the leg. He bound his wound before he passed out. Restless, his horse broke away and returned home. A search party found Janda the next day, but he died two weeks later. His son Joseph (right) was born in 1865. He was a farmer, an organizer of the state KJT (Catholic Union of Texas), and an active member of the Holy Rosary Catholic Church. Janda's son Frank (below), born in 1863, became the first secretary of the state KJT.

SVOBODA.

DEMOKRATICKÝ TÝDENNÍK, HÁJÍCÍ ZÁJMY ČECHO-SLOVANŮ V AMERICE.

ENTERED AS SECOND CLASS MATTER DECEMBER 21, 1908 AT THE POST-OFFICE AT LA GRANGE, TEXAS, UNDER THE ACT OF CONGRESS OF MARCH 3, 1879.

La Grange, Texas. February, 6. 1913.   (Vol. XXVIII. No. 6.

Many immigrants who arrived in La Grange were more comfortable speaking their native tongue; thus, many businesses worked to accommodate the newcomers. The Czech newspaper *Svoboda* was established in 1887, while the German *La Grange Deutsche Zeitung* began publication in 1896. Many La Grange merchants advertised their wares in three languages in order to attract customers. Shown here are the February 6, 1913, issue of the *Svoboda* and the March 13, 1924, edition of the *Zeitung*. (Both courtesy FPLMA.)

La Grange Deutsche Zeitung

Special-Organ der Deutschen in Fayette - und den umliegenden Counties

Jahrgang 34.   LaGrange, Fayette County, Texas, Donnerstag, den 13. März 1924,   Nummer 31.

INLAND

Four

WORKING HARD AND
PLAYING HARD

Between its founding in 1837 and the start of the Civil War, La Grange worked hard as a mercantile center supplying area plantations and as the seat of county government. By 1860, La Grange was supporting nearly 1,000 Fayette County farms, which produced more than 12,000 bales of cotton and 320,000 bushels of corn, along with tobacco and wool.

By the start of the 20th century, when immigration had helped Fayette County reach an all-time high in population (36,542), La Grange was a bustling little city of 2,392. It boasted one wholesale grocery business; seven general merchandise stores; four groceries; five dry goods stores; three hardware stores; three furniture houses; two saddleries; two jewelry stores; three drugstores; 11 barrooms; two beer agents; three blacksmith shops; three shoemakers; two tailors; one millinery; two restaurants; three hotels; one lumberyard; two livery stables; two granaries; one marble yard; one English, one German, and one Czech newspaper; 16 lawyers; two dentists; five physicians; two banks; two meat markets; two photograph galleries; one waterworks and electric light plant; one cotton oil mill; one cotton compress; one soda factory; one ice factory; and two cotton gins. These merchants continued to supply farmers of the area.

During the 20th century, agricultural production turned increasingly to raising cattle. By the 1980s and 1990s, area economic development largely relied on natural resources such as construction gravel, grinding pebbles, clays, timber, oil, and gas.

Besides working hard, La Grange citizens played hard. Parades, local stage productions, baseball games, picnics, beer drinking, singing groups, local bands, high school athletics, and church activities have all been popular. By 1900, La Grange had nine fraternal lodges. Having fun while providing a well-needed service or supporting a favorite charity is a hallmark of La Grange. Even today, area organizations continue to hold dinners, festivals, auctions, or other forms of entertainment to raise money for worthy causes.

Cotton was a big cash crop for Fayette County. During the Civil War, it was shipped to Mexico to raise money for the Confederacy and to provide badly needed supplies to civilians. After the war, freedmen worked cotton fields as sharecroppers, receiving one-third or one-half of the crops for their labors. By 1929, more than half of all farmland in Fayette County was planted in cotton, and production averaged 30,000 bales annually. By 1987, however, cotton was no longer grown. (Courtesy FPLMA.)

After the Civil War, plantation owners sold off their land to German and Czech immigrants, an act resulting in smaller, more numerous farms. The rich soil, abundant surface and groundwater, and intensive cultivation caused these farms to be more productive. The small farms turned to truck farming—raising cabbages, tomatoes, potatoes, beans, peas, and turnips. Here farmers toil in the Colorado River Valley around 1907. (Courtesy FPLMA.)

In this 1895 view of the east side of the square, busy La Grange merchants serve the citizens of Fayette County. (Courtesy FPLMA.)

Model T cars are parked in the square on Colorado Street. (Courtesy FPLMA.)

Early travel was long and tortuous. In 1845, the local newspaper the *Intelligencer* advertised new stagecoach service by a four-horse team connecting La Grange to Houston via Washington. The second leg of the trip, from Washington to La Grange, cost $5 ($137.52 in today's dollars) and left on Friday at 1:00 p.m., arriving in La Grange on Saturday at 6:00 p.m. Today the 59-mile trip can be made by automobile in approximately 1 hour and 15 minutes. A stagecoach sits on the north side of the square in 1865, and a team of oxen waits in front of a La Grange hotel in 1860. (Both courtesy FPLMA.)

On New Year's Eve in 1880, the first train of the Galveston, Harrisburg, and San Antonio Railway Company (a subsidiary of Southern Pacific) arrived in La Grange. The town was electrified. Business was suspended, crowds gathered, and 100 guns were fired. The railroad brought many changes in addition to convenience; for instance, immigration swelled. The Southern Pacific depot is pictured here in 1895. (Courtesy FPLMA.)

The Missouri, Kansas, and Texas Railroad (known as Katy and M-K-T) came to La Grange in 1886. The depot, with segregated waiting rooms, an office, and a freight area, was completed in 1897. Passenger service continued until the 1950s, and the depot received and dispatched freight until the 1970s. The M-K-T Depot, seen about 1910, has recently been restored and is now open to the public. (Courtesy FPLMA.)

RECEIVED by the Steamer Kate Ward, and for sale, low for cash the following articles:—

    10 Barrels Whiskey (Rectified,)
    1 Cask Port wine,
    10 barrels Sugar,
    6 boxes Tobacco, superior.
    5 tierces Rice,
    5 boxes Chocolate.
    20 kegs "Duponts F. Powder.
    50 sacks Salt.
    30 Coils Rope.
May 16th–35–tf.   S. WARD.

SUGAR AND MOLASSES.

Because overland transportation was so treacherous, early settlers looked for ways to find cheaper and more reliable transportation. Their focus immediately turned to the Colorado River. The largest river wholly in Texas, the Colorado is about 600 miles long and has a drainage area of approximately 39,900 square miles. In June 1845, the first steamboat to operate on the Colorado River, the *Kate Ward*, was launched. She was described as a side-wheel steamer, 115 feet long and 24 feet wide at the beam, with two engines rated at 70 horsepower each. The May 16, 1846, *La Grange Intelligencer* ran these advertisements for goods having arrived on the *Kate Ward*. The federal government purchased the steamer in 1853, and her ultimate fate remains unknown. (Both courtesy Texas State Library and Archives Commission.)

May 16th–35–tf.   S. WARD.

SUGAR AND MOLASSES.

RECEIVED, by the steamer Kate Ward, on consignment, the following articles, which the subscriber respectfully requests the western merchants to call and see. He intends to sell low for cash,

    47 barrels Molasses.
    12 barrels Sugar.
    8 hogsheads Sugar.
May 16th—35—tf   J. C. ECCLES.

LOST.

The shallow, meandering Colorado River can, at times, become life threatening. The floods of 1869 and 1913 caused misery and havoc. In 1869, water covered the entire square of La Grange and was one inch higher than the 1913 flood. On December 5, 1913, the water was 4 feet high on the courthouse square (above), and three-fourths of the town was underwater, the river having reached a stage of 56 feet. Houses were flattened, and five dead bodies floated through town. Work committees were formed and a curfew of 10:00 p.m. decreed. In the bottom photograph, construction continues on the custom-designed Parker through truss bridge with five spans, which crosses the Colorado on State Highway 71. Completed in 1941, the bridge is on the National Register of Historic Places. Today massive flooding is prevented by a series of dams and lakes built upstream by the Lower Colorado River Authority. (Both courtesy FPLMA.)

STREET SCENE, SCHUHMACHER BANK BUILDING AND HISTORIC OAK, LA GRANGE, TEX

John Schuhmacher was the consummate entrepreneur who delivered what his clients wanted. He ran a general store that was popular with the German and Czech immigrants because their native languages were spoken. In 1886, he opened a private bank that allowed cotton growers to pay their bills only once a year by extending credit to town merchants, who in turn extended it to the farmers. The business incorporated in 1909 under the name John Schuhmacher State Bank and continued to operate independently until being purchased in 2006. Other Schuhmacher ventures included a wholesale grocery, telephone company, and beer distribution company. The bank building (above, far right) is pictured here around 1907, along with a bank teller in a teller cage (below). (Both courtesy FPLMA.)

La Grange was the first city in Texas to established rural free delivery of the mail. After rural free delivery was inaugurated in 1896, La Grange postmaster H. C. Heilig had a route mapped out. A petition with the required number of signatures was obtained, and delivery began in 1899. The route was approximately 23 miles long and served 685 people. Adolph Giessel (above) worked as the first rural mail carrier. John L. Giese (right) prepares for delivery in his automobile. (Right courtesy FPLMA.)

Poor or nonexistent roads were a problem in the 19th and early 20th centuries, with wet weather making them virtually impassible. Oxcarts hauling three bales of hay, for instance, could only travel a few miles a day. During the 1800s, local citizens were assigned portions of Fayette County country roads to maintain along with help from their neighbors. H. L. Kreische maintained the road from La Grange to Schulenburg that ran by his brewery, building elaborate stonework bridges over creeks and ravines. The top image shows work on a town road in 1929, while the other depicts public roadwork near O'Quinn, Fayette County, in 1895. (Both courtesy FPLMA.)

The Heintze Speckels Store was located in La Grange. (Courtesy FPLMA.)

H. G. Gerdes's Grocery sold staples and fancy groceries. At this La Grange establishment, one could purchase food for farm animals as well as for humans. (Courtesy FPLMA.)

African American women such as the one pictured here frequently found work as domestics or laundresses. (Courtesy FPLMA.)

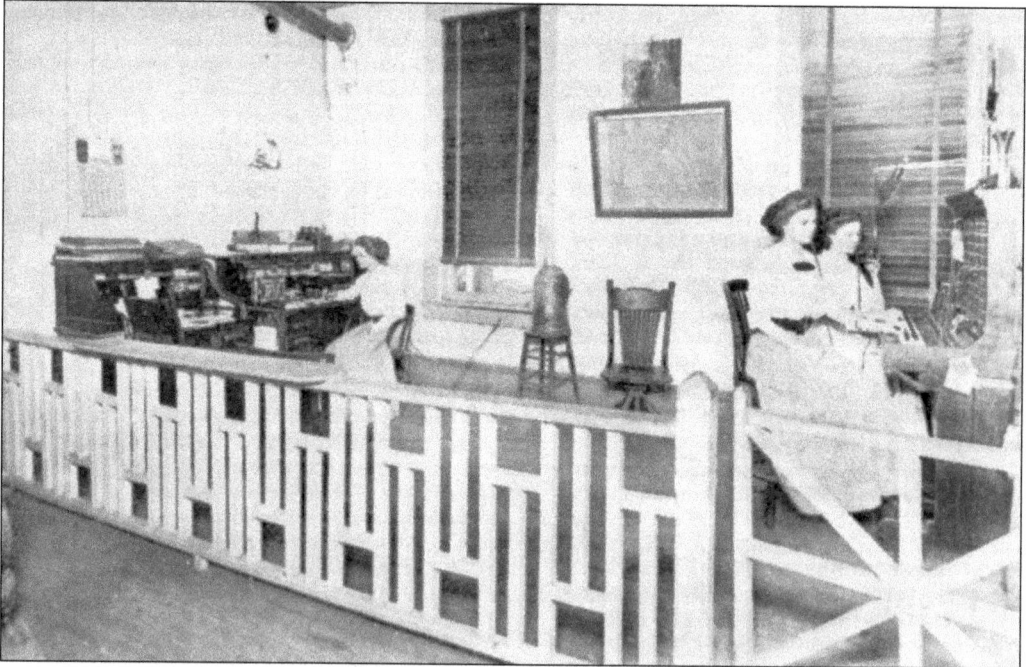

Early in the 20th century, the Schuhmacher Company started the first telephone exchange in La Grange with offices located above the Schuhmacher Bank. Telephone operators are seen here in 1908.

The Schuetzen Pavilion, situated on the bluff above the Colorado River, was a popular place to relax, hold special receptions, celebrate holidays, dance, and drink Kreische's Bluff Beer. H. L. Kreische built the pavilion around 1870, and it saw its last function in 1923. Although the pavilion is no longer standing, visitors can still enjoy the view and a picnic on the bluff at the current Monument Hill and Kreische Brewery State Historical Site. (Courtesy FPLMA.)

The crown jewel of the Fayette County fairgrounds is the pavilion or roundup hall, built in 1925 and pictured in 1938. The hall's high-pitched ceiling and louvered windows coaxed a breeze onto the pine dance floor. Over the years, partygoers have enjoyed music from entertainers such as Ernest Tubb as well as parties, wedding feasts, and other types of gatherings. The hall still sports brown metal baby cribs—a reminder of an earlier era when families came to events together and the younger children were put to bed in the cry room while their parents had fun. (Courtesy FPLMA.)

La Grange men found the saloon a haven in which to play cards or just relax with a beer. (Both courtesy FPLMA.)

Church members enjoy an ice cream social on the grounds of the courthouse around 1894. (Courtesy FPLMA.)

Liane de Lassaulx Tuttle celebrates her birthday with friends at the Opera House on February 28, 1908. (Courtesy FPLMA.)

Game abounds in the rural areas around La Grange. A deer hunter shows off his kill near O'Quinn Creek in 1883, while fox hunters are mounted and ready for the chase. (Both courtesy FPLMA.)

FISHING IN THE COLORADO RIVER, LA GRANGE, TEX.

Fishing is another treasured pastime of La Grange residents. A small craft maneuvers the Colorado River on a c. 1907 fishing expedition. Percy Faison displays his catch. (Both courtesy FPLMA.)

High school sports continue to be popular for players and spectators alike. Shown here are the 1938 championship La Grange football team (above) and the 1936 La Grange pep squad. (Both courtesy FPLMA.)

Baseball has been a staple in La Grange whether it is played in organized teams, as pictured above in the early 1900s, or as a pickup game in the pasture. (Both courtesy FPLMA.)

The Handel Club, whose float is seen in a 1907 La Grange parade, was one of approximately seven singing clubs in the La Grange area at the start of the 20th century. Its purpose was to form a more perfect union, establish discipline, provide for the advancement of music, spread knowledge of music history, and establish a familiarity with the lives of the great masters, as well as promote self-improvement and the general welfare of the club and its members. Founded in 1905, the group remained active until around 1938. (Courtesy FPLMA.)

Merchants used every opportunity to advertise their wares, as August Heintze did on this 1902 parade float. (Courtesy FPLMA.)

If singing was not your cup of tea, you could join a band. Pictured here are Knape's Original Concert Band in 1912 (above) and the La Grange Citizen's Band. (Both courtesy FPLMA.)

A women's literary circle intent upon studying Shakespeare and his works organized in 1899 and eventually adopted the name Etaerio, meaning companionship. In 1902, the women decided to start a circulating library and eventually purchased the old Stiehl home (above) for their growing collection of books in 1912. Their meetings continued until 1938, when the club disbanded for lack of interest. At that time, the property and its collection of 1,500 volumes were transferred as a gift to the City of La Grange for use as a public library. (Courtesy FPLMA.)

One of two opera houses in La Grange, this facility opened on November 11, 1890. Located on the corner of Franklin and Colorado Streets, the building was also used for military balls by the Fayette Light Guards. It closed on April 5, 1904. (Courtesy FPLMA.)

Five

THE MIGHTY ARM OF THE LAW

The Fayette County Courthouse and Sheriff's Office are located in La Grange, making the town the center of law and order for the county. The courthouse occupies a prominent position in the town square and continues to be the center of public and business life.

As the principal law enforcement officer of the county, the sheriff protects lives and property, keeps public order, prevents crime, and arrests lawbreakers. The sheriff is also the administrator of the county jail. Additionally, he is responsible for being the executive officer for the district county courts—serving all their writs, subpoenas, summonses, and processes.

Before laws enforcing the rights of prisoners and setting standards of behavior for law enforcement officials were enacted in the 1970s, Texas sheriffs had an uncommon amount of authority with which to perform their duties. It was typical for the high sheriffs, as they were known, to use their knowledge of the community and informants to come up with a suspect and then to interrogate the suspect until a confession was made.

With this unprecedented power came danger and rugged living conditions. The period from 1840 to 1910 was a particularly dangerous time to be a sheriff in Texas. Political conflicts, family feuds, and vigilantism put his life at risk. Because the office of high sheriff was an elected position, the sheriff had to develop a Jekyll and Hyde personality—he had to be mean to the bad guys so they would not settle in the county and approachable to the law-abiding citizens so he could be reelected. The necessity of winning the public vote forced these sheriffs and their deputies to be the county's "fix-it" men.

In 1855, Heinrich L. Kreische built the third county courthouse, shown here. By 1889, a Fayette County grand jury deemed it in poor condition and recommended a new courthouse costing between $65,000 and $90,000. Scandal erupted when naysayers pointed out the following: the adequacy of the old courthouse, the new courthouse's location in a flood plain, the absence of competitive bidding, the astronomical architect fee, and the excessiveness of the plans. Despite objections, the old courthouse was demolished in 1890. To the delight of the naysayers, the building was so stable that it had to be blown apart with "dynamite and giant powder," according to the *La Grange Journal*. (Courtesy FPLMA.)

James Rieley Gordon was 28 years old when he designed the Fayette County Courthouse. He just happened to be at the meeting in Fayette County approving construction of the new courthouse and quickly sketched his ideas for the ground floor. Shortly thereafter, he won a medal of merit for his design for the Texas Building at the World's Columbian Exposition in Chicago (1892–1893). Gordon went on to design hundreds of structures all over the country, including the Arizona State Capitol. (Courtesy FPLMA.)

The cornerstone for the new courthouse was laid on April 9, 1891, to the pleasure of the 2,000 spectators who came from all parts of the county for the event. After the speeches, the crowd headed to the park, where they consumed a dinner of barbecue beef, mutton, and pork supplemented by pickles and coffee. Women were served first, and the *La Grange Journal* complained that the men, when at last allowed to fill their plates, rushed the food, causing a free-for-all. At least, the *Journal* stated, no men were observed drunk at the opera house where the Blackjack Brass Band played that evening. The courthouse opened in November at a cost of $99,407.04 (about $2 million in today's dollars). The Romanesque Revival building was constructed with blue Muldoon sandstone, Belton white limestone, Pecos red sandstone, and pink Burnet granite. (Courtesy FPLMA.)

The courthouse was built with a 30-by-30-foot uncovered atrium, as shown here in 1894. Warm air was drawn out of the offices surrounding the atrium, cooling them during the summer. This structure worked well in the hot months, but in the winter, the hallways around the atrium could become icy during cold spells. By 1949, the atrium was closed to make room for more vault and office space and general storage. Courthouse renovations in 2005 uncovered and restored the atrium to its original splendor. Although James Rieley Gordon put atriums in other courthouses, this is believed to be the only one recoverable. (Courtesy FPLMA.)

Born in Virginia, James Seaton Lester moved to Texas in 1834 and fought with Colonel Moore against the Native Americans. He later became a recruiting agent for the Texian army in Bastrop, where he reportedly met David Crockett and his men. Lester was supposedly responsible for sending them to defend the Alamo. His service history is extraordinary—five-time congressman of the Republic of Texas, early trustee of Baylor University, chief justice of Fayette County from 1844 until 1848, and member of the Texas Veterans Association. Lester died a bachelor and was buried in La Grange in 1879. (Courtesy FPLMA.)

One of the most notable members of the clergy was Robert Emmett Bledsoe "R. E. B." Baylor. At age 46, the Kentuckian moved to Texas and settled in the La Grange area. In 1841, he became a member of the judiciary. Continuing to serve as a judge until 1863, he held court by day and preached by night. As a Fayette County delegate to the Convention of 1845, Baylor helped to write the first state constitution. Perhaps his biggest accomplishment was as a founding member of Baylor University, where he served on the board and taught law occasionally without pay. He died a bachelor at Gay Hill in 1873.

Judge Livingston Lindsay had a long career teaching school and practicing law before moving to La Grange at the age of 54 to join his daughter, who had married the popular Confederate hero Ben Shropshire. One Monday morning about 9:00 in August 1867, Lindsay got into a confrontation with Dr. J. P. Brown in front of G. Friedberger's store and stabbed Brown. Although Lindsay was summoned to the magistrate's court and posted bond, he apparently suffered no further punishment, as he took his seat on the Texas Supreme Court on September 10, 1867. He was appointed to the Supreme Court by the occupying Union forces because of his moderate views and his disdain for slavery, which inflamed local residents. In 1868, area blacks belonging to the Loyal League marched into La Grange—military style and armed—to vote. When asked why they came to town in this fashion, they answered that Judge Lindsey had advised them it was necessary for their protection. Lindsay served on the court until 1869, when the number of justices was reduced to three. His last official position was Fayette County judge. He died in La Grange in 1892.

Matthew Gaines, a Washington County resident and former slave, was elected as a senator to the state legislature in 1869. Gaines supported the successful legislation for a Texas land grant college, which resulted in the formation of Texas A&M and Prairie View A&M Universities. Not everyone appreciated his efforts. In 1871, he was indicted by the grand jury at La Grange for bigamy and convicted in 1873. The Texas Supreme Court overturned his conviction, but his political career was over. He died in Giddings in 1900.

At the age of 26, John Hancock was elected judge of the Second Judicial District of Texas, which encompassed Fayette County. He established order in the court, telling the lawyers, witnesses, and jurors they better be present when court started or they would be fined. Hancock frequently heard cases involving violations of gaming laws. It was common practice to turn those convicted loose and let them settle their fines when they pleased. Judge Hancock stopped this practice, requiring violators to pay up or go to jail. He retired from the bench in 1865. (Courtesy Library of Congress.)

White Texans used various tactics to keep their black counterparts from voting: enacting a poll tax; establishing polling places far from black communities; blocking bridges and roads on election days; and relocating polling places at the last minute. Despite these strategies, the black citizens of La Grange actively participated in politics. On March 22, 1919, African American citizens gathered to determine how they would vote on the constitutional amendments on the upcoming May ballot. Pictured above is the Republican county convention held in the courthouse in La Grange on July 16, 1904, and attended by approximately 200 blacks. The white men are spectators. (Courtesy FPLMA.)

The first jail in La Grange opened in 1838 but was later sold, and prisoners were parceled out to citizens for incarceration. This worked well until a murderer needed to be imprisoned. A second jail was built in 1853. Soon the county commissioners determined a new jail was in order, and the facility pictured here was completed in 1883. Now known as the Old Fayette County Jail, it was in continuous use until 1985. (Courtesy FPLMA.)

In days gone by, La Grange drunks were put into one of two hoosegows overnight and let out in the morning. The floors were covered with straw, and the inebriated citizens were allowed to sing, yell, and carry on to their hearts' content. It was not uncommon for nearby residents to hear the ruckus on hot summer nights when their windows were opened wide in an attempt to catch a cool breeze. (Courtesy FPLMA.)

Sheriff August Loessin, it is said, garnered respect by using his fists and brought the county a reputation for law and order. Born in Prussia, he came to the United States with his parents when he was three weeks old. Loessin served as Fayette County sheriff from 1894 until 1920. He and his wife, Louise Stegemann, lived at the old jail, where Louise had the responsibility of feeding the prisoners. As sheriff, Loessin was responsible for hanging two men convicted to death during his tenure. (Courtesy FPLMA.)

Cattle rustling was big business in Fayette County. Charles Hendrickson Null, constable of Precinct No. 5 of Fayette County and the owner of a large herd of cattle, had discovered evidence that he felt could put somebody in the penitentiary. Null told others his life was in danger and that he expected to be killed. Then, on August 8, 1896, while riding to the precinct courthouse in Muldoon, he was ambushed by several men. The bushwhackers shot him three times and, while he was on the ground, once more in the head. Sheriff August Loessin immediately suspected Bunk Stagner, whose family was mixed up in cattle theft, because he found tracks of Stagner's mule nearby. About a month later, Null's son, Will, confronted Stagner and emptied both barrels of his shotgun into the man, killing him; Will was tried but never convicted.

To The
Hanging —
ADMIT ONE.

Aug Loessin
Sheriff. F.

The old jail saw two hangings take place on its grounds. Clay Ford, an African American, was hanged on July 20, 1899, for the beating murder of an elderly black woman and the beating of her grandchild during a robbery. By 10:00 a.m. that day, the streets and jail yards were full of onlookers. A prayer was said, a song was sung, a black cap was put over his face, and the trap was lowered. John Boyd, also African American, was accused of raping a pregnant Czech woman. While Deputy Will Loessin was questioning Boyd in Schulenburg, a crowd gathered, ready to lynch him. Deputy Loessin hustled the prisoner away without the mob's knowledge so he could have his day in court. Before Boyd was hung on January 8, 1909, it is said that he ordered the minister to leave (saying he did not need any religion), walked upon the scaffold, made a short talk to the other black people who had gathered to watch, and then said he was ready to go. (Courtesy Old Fayette County Jail.)

William Loessin, known fondly as "Mr. Will," began his law enforcement career in 1895 as deputy sheriff under his brother August. Beginning in 1900, he served as the city marshal of La Grange until he was elected sheriff of Fayette County in 1924. Mr. Will carried a .45-caliber silver six-shooter with gold inlay work and pearl handles that was presented to him by the people of La Grange. Since he had to depend on the vote to continue as sheriff, he handled Prohibition tactfully—in a way the citizens could tolerate. Mr. Will looked the other way when residents produced alcohol for personal consumption, but if they made it to sell, he gave them a warning. They had a week to dismantle the still. If he found they had not complied, he would bust up the still and possibly arrest them. Mr. Will retired in 1947. (Courtesy FPLMA.)

By the time Raymond Hamilton stood trial in La Grange in May 1933 for robbing the Carmine State Bank in Fayette County, he had already been tried five times, convicted four times, and assessed sentences totaling 65 years. By far the most dangerous criminal ever locked up in the old jail, Hamilton began his prolific life of crime as a member of the infamous Bonnie and Clyde gang. He was executed on May 10, 1935, at the age of 22.

Six

THE GOOD, THE BAD, AND THE UNLUCKY

Like any community, La Grange had its share of citizens who ran the gamut from brave and courageous to downright kooky. In the early days, it took fortitude and a strong constitution to survive the hardships of frontier life. Arguments were often settled with fists, knives, or guns—even by civic leaders and the well-heeled. Dueling, for instance, though strictly forbidden, was popular in Texas. On June 12, 1845, Charles F. Augustus "Gus" Williams, who represented Fayette County in the House of Representatives of the Ninth Congress (1844–1845), killed Fayette County sheriff Aaron A. Gardinier in a duel over a political race. No action was taken against Williams, who the very next year represented Goliad in the House of Representatives of the First Legislature of the State of Texas.

Violence also touched families. Samuel Brown, the son of Dr. J. P. Brown, chased his wife out of the house on a May morning in 1881. Despite pleas from his eight-year-old daughter, he slashed his wife's throat with his razor and then took his own life. In 1891, Mathilde Homuth Rethke saw her brother Fritz Homuth shot down by his longtime friend John Rankin, a county clerk. Rankin claimed self-defense and served no time. A few months later, Mathilde's husband, a butcher, shot his new meat cutter in the arm near the elbow.

And what town would be complete without its share of dirty rotten scoundrels? La Grange had a few. Michael and John Short arrived in Texas in 1835 and settled in southwest Fayette County, where they farmed and operated a mill. Although they championed the abolition of slavery and began an Underground Railroad, it seemed runaways were getting caught and resold again and again. Though never proven, it was rumored that the Shorts made money on each transaction. Soon Short descendants were branching out to cattle theft and a counterfeiting ring involving five states.

Meanwhile, Michael Short's wife, Permelia, asked for a divorce in 1847 because Michael would not help support the family, was verbally abusive, and finally abandoned the family. Michael accused his wife of forcing him to live in the outhouse. The county granted the family a small sum, and Michael was eventually given land rights and a small pension for being at San Jacinto even though there was no proof he had even fought in the battle.

According to family legend, Henderson Martin was born in 1866 and grew up on land owned by a white man named Martin Liggons. Around 1891, Martin rode his horse to La Grange and tied it up near the feed store. A white man walked up to Martin and told him that black newcomers in town had to show the townspeople how good they could dance before they could walk around. The man drew his pistol and yelled, "I said dance, nigger, dance," and shot at Martin's feet, making him dance. By that time, a crowd had gathered and Martin was humiliated. He told the white man it was his turn to dance. When the man approached, Martin drew a short rifle out of his waistband and shot him in the chest. Quickly Martin mounted his horse and rode to the Liggons ranch. A posse followed, but because Liggons was known to have killed several men himself, the posse turned back and Henderson was never bothered again. Martin later inherited 2,000 acres of land from Liggons and became a prosperous farmer. When oil was found on the property, the family became extraordinarily rich. (Courtesy Rick Hyman.)

In 1895, *Norma Trist: A Story of the Inversion of the Sexes* scandalized Texans. The novel, set in La Grange, is considered to be the first to deal with the topic of homosexuality. About a lesbian heroine who is cured of her unnatural passion by an alienist, the tale features the Muster Oak, the tomb of the Mier and Dawson soldiers, and Kreische's house. Its author, John Wesley Carhart, M.D., moved to La Grange in 1894 to practice medicine. His career was as colorful as his choice of subject matter. Born in New York in 1834, Carhart started his career as a Methodist minister. While functioning as a minister, he began to practice medicine, write poetry, essays, and biographies, and eventually earned his doctor of divinity. While in Racine, Wisconsin, he invented the first vehicle in the United States to travel under its own power—the "Spark," which ran on steam. Upon the publication of *Norma Trist*, he was arrested at his home and charged with "sending obscene literature through the mail" but later released and his case dismissed. Carhart passed away in San Antonio in 1914.

Before welfare checks, there was the poorhouse. Established in 1881 to care for indigents, the poorhouse was located about two miles east of La Grange. Awarded the contract, John Rankin was paid $11.50 a month to care for up to 10 people and allowed $9 for each person he buried. The county additionally supplied the residents with all the bacon they could eat. At least once a week, they received molasses and biscuits. The editor of the *La Grange Journal* glowed about the facility: "We could not but congratulate ourselves and the community upon the good appearance presented by this institution of charity in our midst and feel impressed with the results of an enlightened and Christianized world." (Courtesy FPLMA.)

Ira G. Killough had the father-in-law from hell. Born in Tennessee in 1830, Killough came to Texas in 1851 and married Tabitha Bowen Moore, the daughter of John Henry Moore, three years later. He farmed, raised stock, speculated in real estate, and participated in the Presbyterian church. On October 2, 1878, Killough was riding in an open buggy with his wife and youngest son. The family met three of Tabitha's relatives armed with double-barreled shotguns. From three feet away, John D. Hunt shot Killough, killing him instantly. Hunt was tried and acquitted, but no charges were ever filed against the other two. Hunt and his wife, Mary, Tabitha's sister, soon moved out of the county to other property owned by John Henry Moore. Local legend states that John Henry did not like Killough and so coerced Hunt to kill him.

Former slave Dave McKinney, along with the rest of the African American population of La Grange, was paralyzed with fear. An ax murderer was loose in Texas, preying on black families. In April 1912, black residents were murdered in San Antonio and Hempstead. In nearby Colorado County, six blacks were killed in their sleep. McKinney secured an old army rifle to protect his loved ones. Local whites caught sight of him and, mocking him, took him to the photographer, where this portrait was taken. (Courtesy FPLMA.)

Little Nellie Mann was playing by the hearth at her home at Christmastime in 1897 when her dress caught fire. She died on January 3, 1898. Distraught, her parents built a Victorian playhouse to cover her grave in the old La Grange Cemetery. (Courtesy author.)

Born in Houston in 1870, Annie Webb Blanton attended school in Houston and La Grange and graduated from La Grange High School in 1886. In 1888, she moved to Austin and taught while attending the University of Texas. Blanton later became the first woman in Texas to be elected to statewide office with the help of newly registered women voters such as this Travis County group. Her tenure as state superintendent saw the implementation of a system of free textbooks, revised teacher certification laws, and increased teachers' salaries. She remained a professor of education at the University of Texas the rest of her life. Before her death in 1945, Blanton had written a number of books and served as vice president of the National Education Association.

Working in the United States at the beginning of the 20th century was dangerous. On May 30, 1912, Edwin Reiss, also known as "the Crowbar Kid," was pinching a wheel of a railcar full of marble from underneath with a crowbar. This is a process whereby the crowbar is put between the wheel and the track and then leveraged in order to move the car. The car moved, but the end of the bar slipped to the ties, and the weight of the moving car forced the upper end through Reiss's abdomen and then through the floor of the car. He was rescued and attended by a local doctor, who sent him to the hospital in Temple in a special railroad car. The doctor in Temple pronounced that the crowbar had missed all of Reiss's internal organs, and the patient made a full recovery. (Courtesy FPLMA.)

She is "a great scould & termagant," claimed first husband Jesse Robinson when he filed for divorce in 1843 from Sarah Jane Newman. "Sally," who came to Fayette County at the age of six, married Jesse at 16. Later she married George Scull (or Skull) and was known by that name for the rest of her life. She was a horse trader and rancher. During the Civil War, she hauled cotton to Mexico and returned with vital supplies for the Confederacy. Known to carry gold coins in a nose bag draped over her saddle horn, Sally is believed to have been killed in a robbery sometime after the Civil War, possibly by her fifth husband. (Courtesy University of Texas San Antonio's Institute of Texan Cultures, No. 103-0266.)

Olga (left), Agnes (center), Ella (right), and Hattie Kruschel were four of seven children born to German immigrant Charles Kruschel and his wife, Emma. Charles built a fine house on North Main, and the sisters lived there until the last one died in 1976. They never married. Their legacy was their philanthropy. They helped finance a community swimming pool and loaned money to save the Faison House. (Courtesy FPLMA.)

Originally from Germany, William Hermes practiced medicine and entered the pharmacy business. At the start of the Civil War, he fled to Nicaragua, then Panama, and eventually to Germany. He returned to La Grange after the war and reopened the drugstore. His wife and child died during the yellow fever epidemic of 1867, but he remarried and began another family. Hermes's drugstore continued after his death in 1922 and is still in operation today. (Courtesy FPLMA.)

Weeds flourished among the bedclothes infected with yellow fever that scattered the town. From July 1867 to January 1868, the local government ceased to function—prisoners in the county jail were either removed or discharged. Citizens fled. The dead were not even given a decent burial, as the supply of caskets had run out. Bodies stood in piles within the cemetery fence, and mass burials took place with six or seven bodies per grave. By the time the plague lifted, one-fifth of the population was dead. Shown here are the graves of William Hermes's first wife and child. (Courtesy author.)

In 1882, Fayette County bought a 450-pound iron statue of a red stag to grace the courtyard grounds along with a dog. The dog was posed as if it were chasing the stag. A number of years later, a group of pranksters broke off the deer's antlers and used them to thrash the dog as punishment for its inability to catch the deer. The dog, alas, did not survive. Throughout the years, well-meaning citizens have replaced the broken antlers with real deer antlers. Although the deer has been refurbished a number of times, vandals have been quick to pilfer the horns and have attempted to make off with the head. The stag has even been shot with small-caliber bullets! In 1999, new horns were attached resembling those of the native white-tail deer. Finally, in 2005, the deer had a thorough restoration and was placed in the atrium of the courthouse, where it is safe from vandals and available for viewing by adoring fans. (Courtesy FPLMA.)

Nathaniel W. Faison came to Texas in the late 1830s, eventually settling in La Grange. The 1840 census indicates he owned one town lot, one silver watch, and one saddle horse. He fought the Comanches with Colonel Moore and survived the Dawson Expedition. Faison held a retail wine and spirits license and served as Fayette County clerk as well as a surveyor, land agent, and factor. During the Civil War, he bought up land from destitute Confederates and, during Reconstruction, donated land to freedmen for a school, church, and cemetery. At the time of Faison's death in 1870 at the age of 52, he owned 35,000 acres and $4,700 in gold, and more than 30 men owed him money. (Courtesy Faison House Museum.)

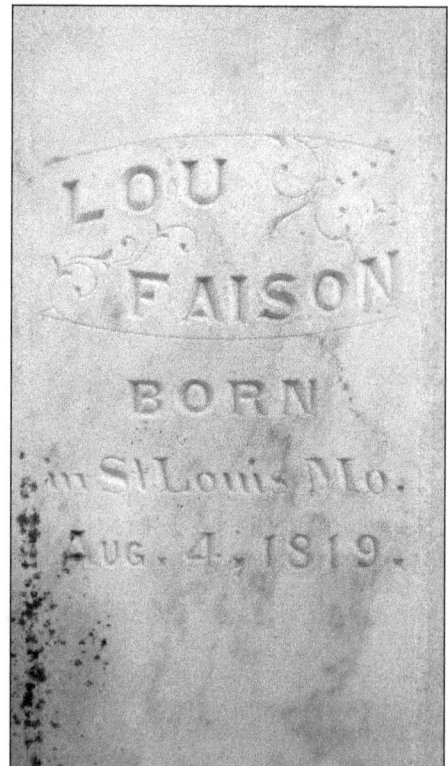

Louisiana Brown, a mulatto, was owned by La Grange merchant James Eccles. By 1870, she was working as the housekeeper for Nathaniel W. Faison. On April 2, 1870, Faison gave her his house, with "all the improvements, household, and kitchen furniture, one buggy, one horse, one pony, and all other stock and personal property of any and every kind now on said premises." Additionally, he left her $3,000 in gold coin. A June 14, 1870, codicil to his will reduced Brown's share of gold to $2,000 and provided Faison's brother Peter with $1,000. By June 29, 1870, Faison was dead. In November 1872, Brown sold the house to Peter. (Courtesy Faison House Museum.)

The inheritance from his brother allowed Peter Faison to live a lavish lifestyle, ordering goods from St. Louis, Missouri, and from Lord and Taylor's in New York. At age 14, Peter's daughter Maria (right) entered a female institute in Virginia. When she became ill, her father ordered her home. She died on March 3, 1888, at the age of 26 after an undisclosed illness. Upon Peter's death, he left more of the estate to his son Jimmie because Peter had repeatedly bailed his son Percy out from under debt. Percy later sued Jimmie over the will when oil was found on the property. Above, Peter and his wife, Susan, sit with Percy (left) and Jimmie (right). (Both courtesy Faison House Museum.)

When the town discovered Teddy Roosevelt would pass through La Grange on March 12, 1911, postmaster August F. Loessin telegraphed his friend Judge Walter Burns with the following: "The city council of La Grange has passed an ordinance strictly prohibiting any ex-president from passing through this city without making at least a five-minute stop. You will please so instruct the Roosevelt committee and warn them against a violation of this ordinance." Burns handed the telegram to Roosevelt, who replied, "By all means let the train stop at La Grange." Indeed, Roosevelt made a short speech from the back of the railcar to a large group of excited, cheering residents. (Courtesy Railroad Museum.)

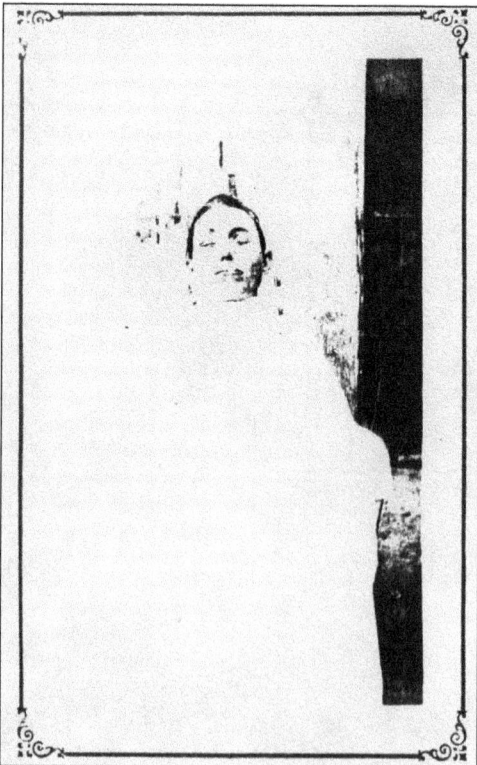

Two men made the mistake of robbing the Carmine State Bank on January 11, 1933, about two months after Ray Hamilton. Leon Addington entered the bank and handed the cashier a note, asking for directions. Then he pulled a pistol and pushed it through the cage. "Stick 'em up," he demanded, forcing the cashier and two others into the vault. The locals alerted Deputy Jim Flournoy, who disarmed the bandit in the getaway car. The deputy then tried the back door but found it locked. The noise he made caused Addington to look away, giving the cashier a chance to shoot and kill the robber. La Grange's Reichert and Kneip undertaking parlor handled the body, and people from all over the county came to view the corpse and take photographs. (Courtesy FPLMA.)

More than 1,000 people gathered on September 18, 1848, to see the remains of the Mier and Dawson Expeditions relocated to the bluff overlooking La Grange. Heinrich Kreische purchased the land the next year and continued throughout his life to keep the vault in good repair. After Kreische's death, the family ceased to care for the tomb. Revelers at Kreische's pavilion, located next to the vault, and other sightseers reportedly viewed and played with the bones, which were exposed by a gaping hole in the tomb. The State of Texas eventually condemned the .36-acre portion of land and took possession of the tomb in 1907. More deterioration occurred until finally, in 1933, a granite vault was erected. In 1936, a 48-foot-tall monument was built to honor the heroes. (Both courtesy FPLMA.)

"Ach, Himmel," murmured the widow Mary Dach ("Oh, heaven," in German) as the deputy explained that she had just been sentenced to death in the electric chair for the murder of her handyman Henry Stoever on February 24, 1933. Despite her contention that Stoever physically and emotionally abused her and her three small children, the all-male jury determined she was just tired of Stoever, whose amorous advances she had previously willingly accepted, and simply wanted a younger man. Her daughter, however, said she was framed by an acquaintance of Stoever's who had threatened to kill the widow's children if she identified him as the culprit. While the widow Dach's case was on appeal, she sat in her cell and read her German Bible until she died of starvation. Today her ghost is believed to haunt the Old Fayette County Jail. (Courtesy Will Loessin estate.)

Seven

THE TRUTH ABOUT THE CHICKEN RANCH

Prostitution was a mainstay of most every Texas town of any importance, including La Grange, in the 19th and early 20th centuries. The Chicken Ranch of Texas legend began in 1915, when Jessie Williams bought property and opened her business on the outskirts of La Grange. Attitudes changed, however, and Texas brothels began closing as the 20th century progressed. The quiet operation in La Grange, on the other hand, continued to operate, in part because of the more tolerant attitudes of Czech and German immigrants toward prostitution.

Its survival also depended on the shrewd business skills of Jessie Williams and the subsequent madam, Edna Milton. The women paid taxes and donated to area charities, all the while purchasing goods from local merchants so everyone had a piece of the economic pie. They did not tolerate drunkenness, sell liquor, or allow minorities to enter the establishment. Cooperation of local law enforcement was essential. County sheriffs in Texas are elected public officials, making their careers dependent on the wishes of citizens. Therefore, rather than shutting down the bordello, the sheriffs managed the brothel and its clientele by ensuring no violence occurred on the premises and by following up on criminal misdeeds reported by Chicken Ranch employees.

The extensive publicity around the closing of "the Best Little Whorehouse in Texas" resulted in a musical and movie of the same name and created many myths about the brothel—to the horror of La Grange citizens.

La Grange, like many towns of the 19th century, segregated prostitutes. An 1897 article in the *La Grange Journal* stated that several of the "soiled doves" had grown weary of their assigned locality, Kalamazoo, about three or four blocks from the courthouse, and had moved into the northeastern part of town. The paper advocated that all "soiled doves" be moved out of the city limits altogether so they would not disturb anyone. The Chicken Ranch of legend began under the tutelage of Faye Stewart, also known as Jessie Williams, of Waco, Texas. She arrived in La Grange about 1913 and bought the property where the Chicken Ranch stands in 1915, owning it until her death in 1962. Miss Jessie's girls, pictured below, were listed as sales ladies in the 1920 census.

114

Miss Jessie finely tuned an ingenious business plan that pacified the local community. Since she established her operation outside of town, the locals were not bothered by the commotion of an all-night business. Her refusal to sell alcohol kept her from competing with the local merchants and avoided problems with the clientele. Not only did she pay taxes and shop locally, but out-of-town clients were apt to stop at a nearby restaurant such as the Old Cottonwood Inn (below) or buy a tank of gas, contributing to the area's economy. The ranch also made charitable donations. Edna Milton gave $1,000 a year for 10 years ($10,000 in 1970, equivalent to $46,000 in 2007) to the community hospital and made contributions to the Little League and swimming pool. Pictured here is an income worksheet for the ranch. (Both courtesy FPLMA.)

EDNA'S RANCH BOARDING HOUSE

Rt. 2, Box 160
La Grange, Texas
Phone 968-3859

INCOME

Date	Room Rent	Board	Beverages	Miscellaneous Sales
1				
2				
3				
4				
5				
6				
7				
8				
9				
10				
11				
12				
13				
14				
15				
16				
17				
18				
19				
20				
21				
22				
23				
24				
25				
26				
27				
28				
29				
30				
31				
TOTALS				

COTTONWOOD INN
DINE — DANCE

Known to all as "Sheriff Jim," Jim Flournoy worked as a deputy, prison guard, livestock inspector, and Texas Ranger before becoming sheriff in 1947. A giant of a man, Flournoy was tough on crime and highly regarded throughout the state. He inherited the relationship between law enforcement and the Chicken Ranch forged by his predecessors. Starting in 1970, he even took mug shots and ran fingerprints on new Ranch employees to ensure they did not have criminal backgrounds. When Flournoy died in 1982, some 400 to 500 people attended his funeral, including 18 cars full of law enforcement officials and the lieutenant governor of Texas, Bill Hobby. (Courtesy Old Fayette County Jail Museum.)

Miss Jessie continued to enlarge the white clapboard house with dark green shutters in a haphazard fashion, adding rooms as needed. Most customers were ordinary citizens—farmers, businessmen, truck drivers, traveling salesmen, military service personnel, politicians, and high school and college students. Texas A&M University students, in particular, were regular visitors to the Ranch (women were not allowed to attend the university until 1964). And yes, the Texas A&M football team did make an appearance. Customers into their 80s frequented the establishment. Minorities, however, were denied entrance. (Courtesy Old Fayette County Jail Museum.)

RULES & REGULATIONS

I, Edna Milton, a femme sole trader own this building and all the furnishings, also 11.32 acres of land duly recorded in the Fayette County Courthouse, La Grange, Texas 78945.

This place nor I have any connections what so ever with an other place mob or syndicate of any type.

This place is individually owned by me.

To whom it may concern to all living on these premises:

If any one here is an illiterate or of sub normal intellig they had better have some one read and explain this to them.

Read this book regularly (about once a month) if you want to live here.

These rules will be followed by all boarders no exceptions

Any one having no intentions of following these rules migh just as will leave now.

Absolutely no narcotics are permitted on these premises if any narcotics are found or suspected the law will be called immediately.

Drinking is not permitted during visiting hours and any on doing so will be asked or ordered to leave.

In short dope heads, pill heads and drunks are not permitt to live here regardless of who they are.

Thieves, liars and robbers are not needed or wanted here when I ask a boarder a question I demand an honest to the point answer.

Edna Milton, a Chicken Ranch employee, bought the establishment from Miss Jessie in 1961 and put her own rules into effect. If the girls went to town, they had to dress reasonably—dresses could be no shorter than two inches above the knees; underwear was required; and pants and shorts were prohibited. The girls worked 21 days on and seven days off. As for their rooms, in which they lived as well as entertained clients, they could decorate any way they chose. The girls usually slept late in their rooms and gathered during the slow afternoons in the private area to visit or read but did not congregate in each others' rooms. Miss Edna did not like cliques gathering and said, "Beds are not to be wallowed in; that is what hogs do." Miss Edna took 75 percent of the earnings, and the girls pocketed the rest. Easter, Thanksgiving, and Christmas were celebrated with large meals, and the girls drew names at Christmas for gift exchanges.

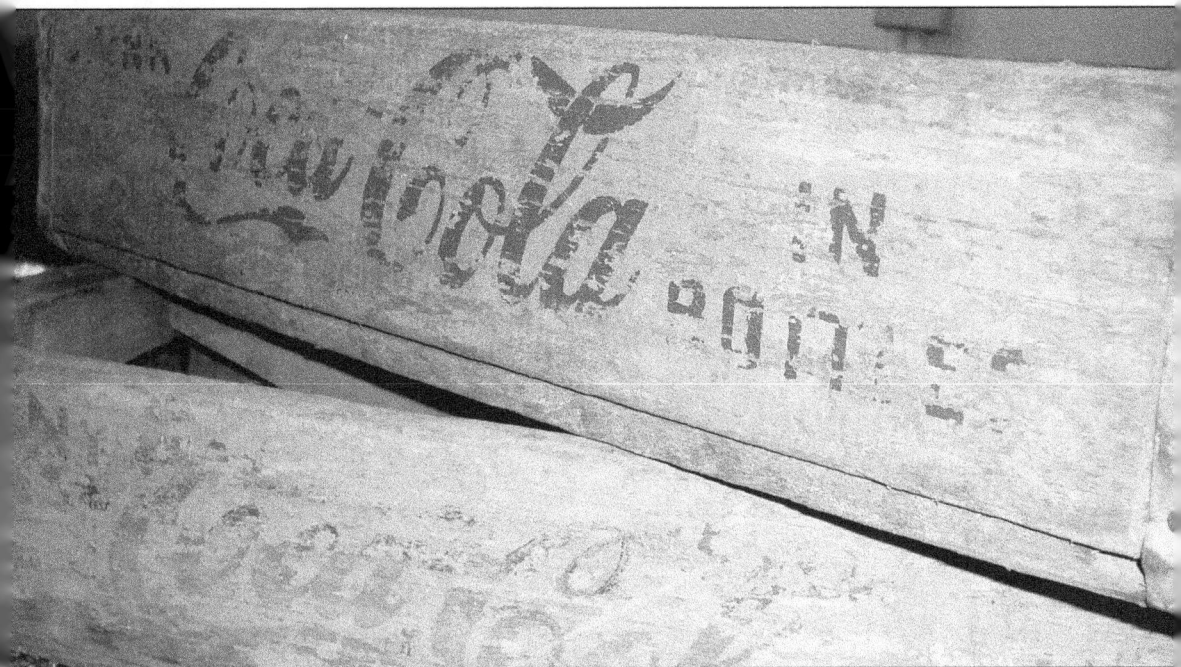

During the late 1960s, a black woman wearing a white maid's outfit would only admit customers she believed to be legitimate. Waiting for admittance was required because there was no handle or latch on the outside of the door. When a customer entered, a bell rang, and the girls came to the front in fancy or scanty attire. Customers and girls gathered in one of the two waiting rooms, which had half-walls so action occurring in both rooms was readily visible. Black vinyl chairs and floor-stand ash trays lined the walls, broken only by an old-fashioned jukebox and Coke machine. A green-and-pink-flowered carpet, complemented by flowered curtains with pink and green sequins, completed the décor. After some small talk, a 50¢ Coke, or maybe a dance, the customer chose a girl, and the two headed to her bedroom to conduct business. The basic rate for a "straight date" was $10 (about $62 in 2007)—cash only. No coins were traded or accepted. Condoms were never offered. For $100, a man could stay all night. (Courtesy Old Fayette County Jail Museum.)

Prostitution is fraught with danger for both the prostitute and the john. Prostitutes can fall victim to pregnancy and physical violence, as well as clients who refuse to pay. Johns run the risk of being robbed. Both parties can contract a variety of sexually transmitted diseases. In the 1960s, the Ranch attempted to lessen these dangers by handling the fee for service and requiring the girls to see a physician weekly. Still, the possibility of violence was ever present. The woman working the door wore a .38-caliber pistol strapped to her thigh, and Miss Edna once fired her .38-caliber Smith and Wesson into the ceiling to impress an unruly customer. In January 1958, Sheriff Flournoy and Deputy Charlie Prilop answered a call from the Chicken Ranch about a robbery in progress. They arrived to find one man stuffing money in a pillowcase while another held a gun over several women tied up in the next room. This .38-caliber Smith and Wesson is similar to the one that protected the Chicken Ranch. (Courtesy Joe Boyle.)

The beginning of the end of the Chicken Ranch occurred when the Texas Department of Public Safety Intelligence Division staked out the bordello on November 17 and 18, 1972. The report estimated that about 484 people entered the premises and that approximately $1.5 million was spent there annually. With this information, Houston television reporter Marvin Zindler backed his allegations that the money from the Chicken Ranch went to bigger organized-crime rings and that local officials were being bribed to allow the operation to continue. All individuals involved—Edna Milton, Sheriff Jim Flournoy, and district attorney Oliver Kitzman—have denied any connection to organized crime or that payoffs were made. (Courtesy Old Fayette County Jail Museum.)

Native Houstonian Marvin Zindler (left) joined the city's ABC affiliate in Houston, Channel 13 Eyewitness News, as a reporter in late 1972, shortly after being fired from the Harris County Sheriff's Office. By July 1973, he was mesmerizing Houstonians on the nightly news with his investigative reporting on the notorious Chicken Ranch and the less well-known Wagon Wheel, outside of Sealy. In a series of nightly reports, he interviewed Sheriff Flournoy, Edna Milton, and even Gov. Dolph Briscoe (below). In later years, he explained his investigation had nothing to do with prostitution, only organized crime. By 1988, Zindler had secured a lifetime contract with Channel 13 and spent the rest of his career championing "the little guy." He died in 2007 at the age of 85. (Below courtesy Texas State Library and Archives Commission.)

Sheriff Flournoy ordered the closing of the Chicken Ranch on the evening of August 1, 1973, in the wake of the furor caused by the television exposé. The closing came at the request of Gov. Dolph Briscoe. Despite accusations by Zindler that the house had reopened, it in fact remained permanently closed.

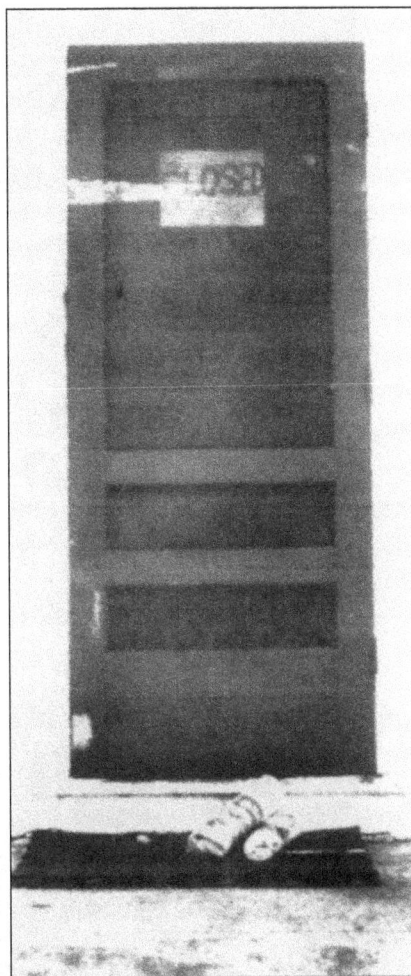

I'm a friend of 'SHERIFF JIM'

Some 18 months after the Ranch closed, Marvin Zindler returned to La Grange to show that the business economy had not suffered. Sheriff Flournoy ran into Zindler and his attorney on the courthouse square. Zindler alleged that Flournoy cursed him, beat his head up against the car door and window, and broke his ribs. Many La Grange residents were secretly delighted when the sheriff grabbed the reporter's hairpiece, waved it around, and threw it in the middle of the street. Zindler later sued for $3 million, creating a groundswell of support for the popular lawman. His supporters displayed bumper stickers such as the one shown, and fund-raisers were held to help pay for his defense. The suit was eventually settled out of court. (Courtesy Old Fayette County Jail Museum.)

Despite the hullabaloo caused by Zindler, the closing of the Chicken Ranch may have faded away save for the band ZZ Top and the sharp wit of Larry L. King. Rock group ZZ Top's first Top 40 hit, "La Grange," was released in the album *Tres Hombres* on July 26, 1973. King, a native Texan, wrote an article for *Playboy* in April 1974 entitled "The Best Little Whorehouse in Texas," regarding the Chicken Ranch and its demise. He then collaborated on a musical of the same name, which opened in 1978 and received a number of Tony nominations and awards. It was followed in 1982 by the movie starring Dolly Parton and Burt Reynolds. Above, Edna Milton stands outside the Broadway theater where the musical ran. She played the small, non-speaking role of the previous madam.

Myths about the Chicken Ranch flourish even to this day. One of the most enduring is how the establishment got its name. Legend states that during the tough times of the Depression, Miss Jessie set up a barter system—one chicken for services rendered. However, during a 1977 interview with the *Dallas Morning News*, Miss Edna told another story. She said that Miss Jessie, afraid of a new grand jury foreman, needed a front for the business. She decided on chickens and bought 100 baby chicks. The property then went on the tax rolls as a poultry farm, and the flock wandered around the place for years. Another popular myth is that coeds from the University of Texas, located 65 miles away, worked there. Not so, declared Miss Edna, who characterized her employees as mostly uneducated unfortunates who were looking for some way to make a living and were only moderately good-looking. (Courtesy author.)

An Editorial:

Time to Close Subject, Too

One reason that so much has been said about the Chicken Ranch in the past week is that so little was said, except covertly, until the place suddenly made the national headlines. The prevailing local attitude was: it's there, it's always been there, it's not doing any harm and, besides, I know practically nothing about it. Our favorite rejoiner, often with a grin, was, "What Chicken Ranch?"

Now everybody knows, from the governor to the myriad fans of Johnny Carson, and everybody in the vicinity has finally had his say.

There is clear indication, by radio poll and personal comment, that the majority of La Grange people strongly disapproved of the place and are thankful for its closing. But the relevant comments of last week are all contained in statements by Governor Briscoe, Attorney General Hill and Sheriff T. J. Flournoy, the first two in that bawdy houses violate state laws and this one must be permanently closed, the latter in that it has been — permanently.

We also have had irrefutable proof this past week as to what the place came to mean for our town. That it was decorously and respectably managed we will accept on the word of the experts. But the fact is that, however fashionable, however philanthropic, a whore house is still a whore house. And when your town becomes known from coast to coast for that one thing, the long-range results are scarcely beneficial. When it comes to be joked about on national television . . . well, it takes a perverted mind indeed to go on saying how good this is for La Grange.

Enough has been said about the Chicken Ranch. It is closed. We should close the subject as well and get on with matters of real worth to our town. And we should make very certain that when some eager outsider asks us in the future we can honestly answer, "What Chicken Ranch?"

Several factors can be attributed to the Chicken Ranch's ability to survive so long. A majority of the local population felt the establishment cut down on rape, teenage pregnancies, and sexually transmitted diseases and enhanced the local economy. After the Zindler debacle, attitudes changed. On August 7, 1973, the *Fayette County Record* wrote, "But the fact is that, however fashionable, however philanthropic, a whorehouse is still a whorehouse. And when your town becomes known from coast to coast for that one thing, the long-range results are scarcely beneficial. When it comes to be joked about on national television, . . . well, it takes a perverted mind indeed to go on saying how good this is for La Grange." That attitude prevails today—the subject is closed. (Courtesy FPLMA.)

Today that "little bitty old piss-ant country place" is nothing to see. Located down a quiet, winding road, the rubble of the Chicken Ranch, shown here in 2005, is unmarked and landlocked. As with many Texas properties, the Chicken Ranch acreage has no public road access. Mother Nature and mankind have conspired to erase any remaining physical vestiges of the past. A portion of the original building was hauled to Dallas in 1977 and transformed into a chicken restaurant, which subsequently failed and was sold in foreclosure. A 1980s attempt to develop the location into a museum and festival site met with strong community opposition and folded. All that remains is a legend.

This is La Grange, Texas—the real capital of Texas. (Courtesy FPLMA.)

Visit us at
arcadiapublishing.com

www.ingramcontent.com/pod-product-compliance
Lightning Source LLC
Chambersburg PA
CBHW050643110426
42813CB00007B/1903